Haunted Delaware

Haunted Delaware

Ghosts and Strange Phenomena of the First State

Patricia A. Martinelli

Illustrations by Heather Adel Wiggins

STACKPOLE
BOOKS

*This book is dedicated with love to three of the most
intelligent, talented, and beautiful young women,
to whom I am privileged to be related: my nieces
Kathryn Noble, Ann Jones, and Sarah Martinelli.*

*They are living proof that the
world is indeed filled with magic.*

Published by
STACKPOLE BOOKS
5067 Ritter Road
Mechanicsburg, PA 17055
www.stackpolebooks.com

Printed in the United States of America

10 9 8 7 6 5 4 3 2 1

FIRST EDITION

Design by Beth Oberholtzer
Cover design by Caroline Stover

Library of Congress Cataloging-in-Publication Data

Martinelli, Patricia A.
    Haunted Delaware: ghosts and strange phenomena of the First State/
Patricia A. Martinelli; illustrations by Heather Adel Wiggins.–1st ed.
        p. cm.
    Includes bibliographical references.
    ISBN-13: 978-0-8117-3297-0 (pbk.)
    ISBN-10: 0-8117-3297-5 (pbk.)
    1. Ghosts-Delaware.   2. Monsters-Delaware.   I. Title.
BF1472.U6M377   2006
133.109749-dc22

Contents

Contents

Introduction

DELAWARE IS ONE OF THE SMALLEST STATES IN AMERICA, SECOND ONLY
to Rhode Island. At just 2,044 square miles, Delaware is smaller
than some counties in neighboring Pennsylvania and New Jersey,
with a length of 96 miles and a width that varies from 9 to 35 miles.
It has major cities such as Dover and Wilmington, where businesses
and traffic jams flourish along superhighways, as well as small
towns such as Pepperbox and Cabbage Corner, which can be discovered tucked away in hidden pockets off winding country roads.
Malls large and small, where millions of dollars' worth of goods are
sold annually, exist side by side with green fields, environmentally
sensitive marshlands, and sandy beaches.

The state's terrain is as diverse as its population. The rolling,
forested hills of the north give way to miles of sandy dunes and
lush, reed-filled marshland along the coast. Inland waterways dom-
inate the landscape in the south. Delaware has the lowest elevation
of any state in the nation; the highest point is 442 feet above sea
level, but most of it sits at about 60 feet.

The sense of age is everywhere—from the broad expanse of
forests where Native Americans once hunted a variety of wild game
to the elegant Colonial-era mansions where the elite gathered
underneath candle-lit crystal chandeliers. Remnants of the past also
include ghost towns, which are sometimes little more than crossroads these days, abandoned cemeteries, and derelict mills. As one
of the oldest settled regions in the country, Delaware has a rich and
colorful history that has produced all types of stories of ghosts, gob-

lins, and other supernatural beings. It doesn't take much imagination—just the right surroundings to feel their presence.

Here, lost children eternally haunt the silent woods. The ghosts of pirates still search the coast for long-buried treasure. Sumptuous mansions like Rockwood and Winterthur are reported to be infested with restless spirits. Hideous monsters lie in wait in the woods for unsuspecting hikers. Throughout the state, the shades of both victims and their murderers have been said to walk the night. Not all of the lore is earthly in origin. UFO sightings have been reported in Delaware since the early twentieth century, long before airplanes, satellites, and other modes of flight became a commonplace sight in the nighttime sky. All in all, there are a number of supernatural tales that will chill the marrow of even the hardiest bones.

To appreciate some of the myths and legends that have been handed down through the generations, it is important to understand a little of the state's history. Picturesque Delaware cuts a small swath out of the eastern seaboard of the United States. It is divided into three counties: New Castle in the north, Kent at the center, and Sussex in the south. The counties were once sectioned into "hundreds," under a system of governance established during English rule to assess taxation. Although these are not officially recognized anymore, residents still commonly use the term to refer to a specific region.

Before the arrival of European immigrants, the Lenni-Lenape shared the land with the Nanticoke, Pocomoke-Assateague, and Nause. These Native American tribes lived in loosely organized settlements along the waterways, traveling primarily during the winter months to hunt fresh game, which included panther, wildcat, and wolf. Today some of the descendants of the Nanticoke have established a small colony in southern Delaware, where they keep alive their native traditions. The descendants of early Swedish, Dutch, and English colonists have long since been joined by immigrants from other nations. The nineteenth century saw an influx of Germans, Italians, and Poles. Greek and Ukrainian immigrants came next, in the twentieth century, and today newcomers include Asians and Hispanics. Many African Americans can trace their heritage to former slaves or free blacks who established lives within the state as early as the 1700s, when they composed about one-fifth of the state's total population.

Although intertribal warfare occurred periodically, the lives of the Natives Americans were not really disrupted until the arrival of European immigrants. Henry Hudson, an explorer in service to the Dutch Crown, is credited with discovering Delaware Bay in 1609, but Thomas Argall, sailing for England, named the territory the following year for Thomas West, better known as Lord de la Warr, the first Colonial governor of Virginia. In the years that followed Hudson's journey, the Native American population watched as Swedish settlers were replaced by the Dutch, who finally ceded ownership of the territory to England. During this period, many tribes moved westward, settling in the region that would eventually become eastern Ohio.

Delaware's future as a colony was still far from secure, however. Further controversy erupted when the land was claimed by both Lord Baltimore of neighboring Maryland and the powerful Penn clan, who had purchased tracts in what would become the colonies of Pennsylvania and New Jersey. The Maryland-Delaware border dispute was settled in 1750 by the British court, but the boundary between Delaware and New Jersey was not finally confirmed until 1935 by the Supreme Court. Even today disputes continue to arise over control of sections of the Delaware River and Bay.

The nickname of Delaware, where the Declaration of Independence was first ratified, is the First State, because it was first to enter the newly formed American Union on December 7, 1787. It was John Dickinson, one of the state's five delegates to the Constitutional Convention, who persuaded his fellow statesmen to draft a new document rather than rewrite the existing Articles of Confederation.

The state is home to a number of prestigious museums and colleges, including the University of Delaware, which pioneered paranormal research in the 1950s. Recreational areas, lush state parks, and vast historic sites draw millions of visitors each year. And Delaware is an acknowledged giant in the world of business. Ralph Nader's Raiders, in fact, dubbed it "the corporate state" in 1973 because so many Fortune 500 companies had established their home offices here. During the past three decades, that number has continued to climb. A recent survey disclosed that more than 183,000 corporations, including forty major American banks, are headquartered here. In addition to its business interests, much of Delaware is devoted to agriculture, with about half of its inland acreage set aside for farming. Among its top crops are soybeans, corn, tomatoes, strawberries, and asparagus, worth approximately $170 million a year.

Then there are the ghosts and strange creatures that haunt the state.

Although ominous-sounding place names like Murderkill, Whorekill, and Slaughter Beach sometimes have reasonable explanations behind them (*kill* is the Dutch word for "river"), Delaware seems to be brimming with supernatural activity. This book offers a sampling of the spectral legends and folktales that have been told in Delaware throughout the years. Some are mildly humorous folktales, and others are strange and truly frightening legends, with an assortment of spirits that range from occasionally benign to, more often than not, those who are seeking to avenge or at least remind others of their violent and untimely death.

As in every region in America that was colonized by immigrants, some Delaware legends have their origins in the folklore of Europe. Banshees, monsters, and demon dogs were just some of the spectral beings who were transplanted to the New World between the seventeenth and twentieth centuries. Spectral orbs, which today are often said to appear where ghosts are present, were once known as *ignis fatuus*, or "foolish fire," supposedly because it was unwise to follow them. They seem to have been a familiar supernatural phenomenon in just about every country in the world. Then there were those pale female figures that haunted the coastline, waiting for their lost lovers to return from the sea. Retelling such tales in new surroundings may have been one way to make the sometimes threatening foreign land seem a little more comfortably like the old. The stories might have been frightening, but at least they were familiar.

Other stories evolved in specific places or as the result of events that occurred to different people at different times in the First State. Although some of the early incidents may seem comical in the twenty-first century, they were often taken very seriously at the time. Remember, there once was only a limited understanding of how the world worked—no science to offer explanations for why storms raged or the farm animals mysteriously took sick and died. Something, someone had to be held accountable, so such misfortunes were attributed to witches who roamed the night or evil monsters that lay in wait to make off with the sheep or sometimes even the children.

To provide the reader with a sense of place, the stories in this book are arranged in chronological order. After all, there is really only one place to begin such a journey—at the beginning, before European immigrants flocked to the newly discovered land that would ultimately become the United States of America. As a result, this book starts in the days of the Native American population and concludes in present times. Whenever a story spans the centuries, it has been assigned to the most appropriate period.

I prefer to be open-minded about these tales and legends, because I have had my share of inexplicable experiences. As far as I am concerned, the world is filled with many things I don't understand, and probably never will. So if the reader's first question is whether the stories are true, all I can say is that it is for each individual to decide. Believers will probably have their faith in the supernatural confirmed, whereas skeptics will continue to doubt. With that in mind, I hope that the tales first and foremost are entertaining and also serve as a reminder that people, places, and things are not always what they seem.

The Early Days

THE COASTAL REGION OF THE NEW WORLD THAT WOULD EVENTUALLY become known as Delaware was a lush, fertile area filled with a variety of natural wonders. The Lenni-Lenape and other Native Americans who lived here fished, hunted, and gathered wild fruits and vegetation from a broad network of streams and forests. Their tranquil lifestyle was ultimately interrupted in 1631 with the arrival of Dutch immigrants, who settled at Zwaanendael, the site of present-day Lewes. However, the folk tales they once related to explain the world around them remain alive, thanks to their descendants who have created a cultural haven for Native Americans in Sussex County.

Native American Tales

The Native American tribes that once populated what is now Delaware spent their days hunting, fishing, and farming the lands along the Delaware River up through the region that would eventually become New York State. On more than one occasion, they had to fight off other tribes that were determined to gain control of the fertile acres they called home. But the real threat to their existence ultimately did not come from those different tribes. It was the arrival of European settlers and their determination to usurp the lands inhabited by the native population that finally proved their undoing.

The clans were organized as matriarchies and usually identified one another by animal signs or totems. They believed in a Great Spirit, who oversaw the Manitou—lesser deities of both good and evil that were present in all aspects of nature. The Native Americans also felt that dreams, visions, and guardian spirits were different means of communicating with the beings that populated the supernatural world. The concept of a Devil was foreign to the Lenape until it was introduced to them by European immigrants.

Although their initial contact with European settlers was marred by bloodshed, they were eventually won over by men like William Penn, who created treaties designed—on paper, at least—to be fair to both sides. The Lenni-Lenape, especially, were very supportive of the colonists during the Revolutionary War, even though the representatives of the future United States of America failed more often than not to keep their promises regarding the Native Americans. As lines of communication opened between these diverse cultures, some settlers made an effort to learn more about Native American traditions.

John Lofland (1798–1849) was an early Delaware resident known regionally as the "Milford Bard." *Delaware: A Guide to the First State,* created in 1938 as part of the Federal Writers Project, notes that he collected Indian legends and "wove them into his romantic stories published in the early nineteenth century but no one today can discover where the legends end and Lofland's vivid imagination begins." Lofland was a drug addict and an alcoholic, and it is likely that the Indian legends appealed to his poetic nature. He documented such tales as the one involving Manitoo, a beautiful Indian maiden who loved a settler, "Wild Harry," of Wilmington. When Manitoo discovered that Harry had been cheating on her, she was said to have been so distraught that she threw herself from a large, flat rock into the deepest part of the Brandywine to end her life. Her spirit reportedly still haunts the region today.

Ultimately, many tribes were pushed west by European settlers, but a small number of the Nanticoke, of the Unalachtigo branch of the Lenni-Lenape, remained in Delaware. Today their descendants are dedicated to preserving their rich history and tribal traditions, which include the folktales of preceding generations. Following are some Native American tales long associated with the Delaware.

The Little Grandfather

A hunter was returning to his village one evening. As he approached, he heard a little voice singing close by. When he investigated the sound, he discovered that the voice was coming from a tiny hole in the ground. The hunter said, "Hey, you down in the hole! Who are you?" The singing stopped, and the little voice replied, "I am a Grandfather, a Spirit. If you wish to learn more, give me some tobacco."

Intrigued, the hunter wrapped some tobacco in a leaf, tied it with a blade of grass, and dropped it into the hole. After a moment, the little voice said, "You are stingy with your tobacco." But it then proceeded to tell the hunter the best story he had ever heard. When it was finished, the little voice said, "Go and tell your people that I will tell a story to anyone who gives me tobacco or a bit of bread. But if you wish to hear another story, don't be so stingy with your tobacco."

This was the beginning of stories told for pleasure. Now this story about stories is ended.

Albino Animals

Almost every Native American tribe related tales about albino animals, which they believed to have a special connection to the spirit world. To them, whiteness was not necessarily associated with purity as it was in the European mind. Instead, it was related to wisdom and ancient knowledge of the world, to which every human should aspire. In addition, it was believed that an albino animal's lack of protective coloring made it an unfair target for pursuit. Bear Two Arrows of eastern Delaware related that anyone who hunted and killed an albino squirrel would suffer the loss of his hunting abilities. If an albino deer were killed without mercy, the hunter might later lose his life in a freak hunting accident.

The Giant Squirrel

The story goes that long ago, Squirrel was huge and went everywhere—in the valleys, woods, and big forests—looking for smaller creatures to eat. He would eat all kinds of animals, even snakes.

One evening, Squirrel saw a two-legged creature running along, so he ran after it. When he finally caught the person, Squirrel snatched him and ate that person all up. Except, that is, for the person's hand, which the giant Squirrel carried with him.

While he was still busy chewing, Squirrel saw an enormous person standing nearby. That person had a very white light shining and shimmering all around him, and when he said anything, he roared like thunder and the earth shook and trees fell down. He was the Creator. The Creator said to Squirrel, "Now, truly you have done a very terrible deed. You have killed my child. From this time on, it is you who will be little and your children and your great-grandchildren will be eaten, and the shameful thing you did will always be seen by a mark under your forearm."

Squirrel was scared and trembled with fear. He wanted to hide the man's hand, and he placed it under his upper arm. This story must be true, because any hunter who has ever prepared a meal of squirrel has seen the hand under the squirrel's upper arm. That is why you should always cut that piece out before cooking the squirrel.

The Good-Looking Woman

Once there was a woman who was so good looking that not only the men but also some of the animals wanted her to fall in love with them. One day, a beaver, an owl, and a skunk were all talking about the woman, and they decided the owl would be the first to take his chances. But when the owl went to see the woman, she told him, "I won't go with you. You are too ugly. Your eyes are too big!" So the owl left and told his friends he had been rejected.

Then the skunk went to see the woman, but he had no luck either. The woman told him, "I won't go with you because you are ugly and you stink." So the skunk went back and told the others about his defeat.

The beaver went next, but he also had no luck. The woman told him, "You are an ugly thing. Your teeth are wide, and your tail is big and broad." When he returned to his friends, they further discussed the matter and decided to get their revenge. The beaver told his two friends that he would gnaw through the log on the riverbank where the good-looking woman went to get water. They were sure that when the log broke and she fell in, the woman would call on them for assistance.

Sure enough, minutes after the beaver had gnawed through the log, the good-looking woman went for water. When the log broke, she fell in and cried, "Now I wish the beaver were here. Maybe he could help me get out of the water." So she began to sing, *"Pe Pe Kwan Sa, Pe Pe Kwan So. Ni ha noliha tamakwesa* [I like the beaver]." But the beaver answered, "No one would like my looks because I am ugly. My teeth are too wide, and my tail looks like a stirring paddle."

Then the woman sang, *"Pe Pe Kwan Sa. Niha nolina shekak-wisa* [I like the skunk]. *Pe Pe Kwan Sa."* But the skunk replied, "No one would like my looks because I am so ugly and because I stink." Finally, in desperation, she began to sing, *"Pe Pe Kwan Sa. Niha noliha kukhusa* [I like the owl]." But the owl answered, "No one would like my looks because I am ugly. I've got big eyes."

So the woman floated on down the creek. Since no one would help her, she finally drowned.

Born in Blood

The relationship between the Lenni-Lenape and European immigrants was forged with difficulty because of cultural differences. In fact, it is a little surprising that the colonists did not completely abandon plans to settle the region, as the first group was massacred about a year after it arrived in the spring of 1631. That was when twenty-eight Dutch colonists landed at Zwaanendael ("Valley of the Swans"), near the site that would one day become the town of Lewes. With high hopes of starting a profitable whaling colony— and arrogance regarding the Native American population—they established a small community on ground that had long been the territory of the Lenni-Lenape.

An uneasy relationship flared into serious trouble after an Indian stole a metal standard bearing the image of a unicorn, the coat of arms of the colonists' native land. Since metal was extremely rare, it seems that he could not resist the prospect of appropriating a piece in order to forge it into a pipe. When the colonists complained to the local chief, he had the thief killed, but this action shocked the Dutch settlers even more. When the thief's relatives learned that the colonists were unhappy with the punishment doled out by the chief, they decided they had had enough of the newcomers and their strange code of behavior. Under the pretext of bringing goods to trade, the Indians arrived at the settlement one afternoon and relentlessly massacred the men as they worked in the surrounding fields.

Imagine the tribe's horror, then, when a new group of colonists landed at the settlement the following year. After spending what seemed like an eternity aboard small wooden sailing ships, they arrived to find the crude cabins and barns standing empty. Instead of a thriving community, they were greeted only by silence. Where could the colonists have gone? The answer to the mystery was soon revealed when they discovered bones of humans and cattle strewn throughout the surrounding fields. It was the remains of the first settlers and their farm animals.

Today the De Vries Monument on Pilot Town Road commemorates the spot along the riverbank where the massacre occurred. It is a popular attraction where many tourists stop on a visit to Delaware. In addition to the marker, the story of that early settlement is told in depth at the Zwaanendael Museum, located a few miles away on Kings Highway and Savannah Road. The now pleasant spot is not as serene some nights as it appears during the day, however. On moonlit nights, some local residents say that you can hear the sounds of galloping hooves and war cries echoing through the dark as the Indians still battle their unwelcome new neighbors to the death.

The Murderkill

The Historical Society of Delaware, a treasure trove of information on the First State's past, includes a scrapbook of newspaper clippings attributed to Mary Briggs of Frederica that is believed to be dated September 10, 1870. According to one article, "Murderkill, Murther Kiln, Murther Creek (also known as Mother Kill), so has this creek or river which contributed to the prosperity of Frederica been called. Legend says that mouth of the river was the scene of a terrible murder in Indian times."

A crew of Native Americans was said to have been drafted by European settlers to pull a cannon along the water's edge, when the "engine of death, loaded with balls and pieces of iron, was fired into them mowing them down as wheat before a scythe. So the hundred and the creek took its name from this inhuman crime."

The Witches of Delaware

Although the witchcraft trials of Salem, Massachusetts, dominated public attention in early America, other colonies sometimes found it necessary to investigate charges of supernatural activity among the immigrants settling in their portion of the New World. In an era when all non-Christian activity was suspect, witchcraft was considered a heinous crime that was often punishable by death. Everyone believed witches gained their powers by consorting with the Devil, so they deserved this fate. Fortunately for some of the suspected witches, most communities in Delaware were not gripped by the same level of hysteria as Salem.

In an article titled "The Ghosts of Southern Delaware" in the October 1979 issue of *Delaware Today,* David S. Hugg notes that three early Delaware residents were tried on charges of witchcraft in the seventeenth century. Two Finnish immigrants, Karen and Lasse, were accused by no less a personage than the region's Swedish governor, John Printz. Their property was confiscated, and they were banished from the colony. A number of years went by with few reports of supernatural activity, but during William Penn's time, according to Hugg: "A woman . . . was taken to court on charges of bewitching her neighbor's livestock. While there is no existing record as to the disposition of the case, it is assumed that she was banished from Penn's 'Three Counties on the Delaware.'"

Ironically enough, some early Sussex County settlers used mystical means to try to remove suspected witches from their midst. Some fired silver shot at a hand-drawn picture of the witch, believing this would cause their human target real physical harm. In other instances, the witch's belongings were destroyed in an effort to make her go away. Their efforts to rid the region of supernatural activity must have been fairly successful, since Delaware's witch hunts never seemed to generate the same degree of fear as those in Massachusetts. Either that or the real witches were able to use their powers to stay out of harm's way.

The Headless Dutchman

Just south of New Castle, visitors can explore the old wooden docks that were built during the seventeenth century. It is probably best, however, to avoid taking any solitary walks in that region at night during the fall. That's when the ghosts of some Dutch soldiers have been seen patrolling the pier, while another—minus his head—marches along the shore. Did they lose a fight with the British or one of the local Native American tribes? If the ghosts know the answer to that question, they're not talking.

Red-Haired Rosie

New Castle, the oldest town in the Delaware River Valley, lies nestled along the Delaware River just six miles—but light years—away from the urban hustle and bustle of Wilmington. Fort Casimir, built there in 1651, is long gone, but traces of the community that sprang up around it remain visible even today. Although signs of modern civilization are present even at the Common, which lies at the heart of the community, they mesh nicely with the brick and wooden Colonial-era homes and businesses that line the brick-paved and cobblestone streets. Local residents take obvious pride in their picturesque town but are almost as proud of the former residents with whom, in some cases, they still share living and working quarters.

That is, as long as it's not late at night, they're not in the basement, and the walls don't seem to whisper in the dark . . .

One local ghost has been christened Rosie because of her flaming red hair. Dressed all in white, she has made her presence known to some of the staff and patrons of The Arsenal, a popular local eatery owned by New Castle resident Richard Day. Drawn to the rich history of the region about ten years ago, Day decided he wanted to share his love of history with both visitors and area residents when he went into business there. As a result, he also opened Jessop's Tavern, a delightful Colonial-style inn on Delaware Avenue. Although he admitted that he personally has never seen Rosie, saying, "I've called out to her but she's never responded," the spirit has been described to him as a tall, young woman with red hair, who appears to be dressed in some type of uniform.

The Arsenal, located behind the historic courthouse at the heart of New Castle, was originally constructed in 1809 to protect the town from British invasion. Used to store ammunition during the War of 1812 and the Mexican War, it also served the community at various times as a school and a hospital. Day believes that Rosie may have been a teacher or nurse who worked there in the early nineteenth century. When she is present in the restaurant's elegant 1812 Room, chairs have been known to move and doors rattle without any apparent help. Rosie also seems partial to the basement and the ladies' room on the second-floor landing.

The spirit of a young boy has also been seen at the restaurant from time to time, but Rosie seems to make the most consistent appearances. Day describes the basement as scary; he believes that yellow fever victims may have been buried there in the early nineteenth century. If this is true, Rosie may have once been a dedicated nurse who even now refuses to be parted from her patients until they too can find rest.

The Fountain of Youth

Famed Spanish explorer Ponce de Leon apparently headed in the wrong direction when he went to Florida searching for the fabled Fountain of Youth. Ask almost any Lewes resident, and he or she will tell you the ancient spring has been located in Delaware all along, just a short ride outside of town on Pilot Town Road. Pilot Town was the name accorded to the area of town that once bordered the southwest bank of Lewes Creek. The pilots who lived at the water's edge had immediate access to their vessels, which allowed them to get out to sea and unload incoming ships faster than their competition. But perhaps they had another reason for living there as well.

According to local legend, the fountain was first discovered by Dutch settlers in 1631, who believed its water could preserve or restore youth, especially if they drank it from a conch shell. Although there are no records showing that the immigrants managed to stay young as they struggled to establish life in the New World, the well remained known for generations as the home of the Fountain of Youth. In 1937, the Lewes Chamber of Commerce constructed a little shelter for the fountain, which still stands today.

The fountain is now supposedly dry, and the conch shell cup is long gone, but it still bears a sign stating, "Private Property, for D.A.R. Member Use Only."

Raiders of the Delaware Coast

Pirates. Even today, it is a word that conjures images of hard-fighting, hard-living men (and sometimes women) who roamed the seas, terrorizing other ships and communities the world over. In early America, they haunted the Atlantic coast from New England to the Caribbean. Pirates became such a problem in Lewes in the late 1600s that an ordinance was eventually passed requiring all residents to own a musket and enough ammunition to help protect the town from future raids. Occasionally, though, the townspeople would just flock to the top of the Great Sand Hill to watch as French and Spanish pirates fought each other or chased down hapless vessels offshore.

Despite the best efforts of the locals, pirates continued to appear along Delaware's coast for many more years. And some say that their spirits are still seen at different points along the shoreline, searching for their buried gold. Legend has it that Captain William Kidd visited Lewes around 1698 and left a treasure chest hidden in the dunes of Cape Henlopen State Park on his way to the West Indies. Kidd, who started his sailing days as a pirate hunter, later came to be known—whether truthfully or not—as one of the fiercest pirates around. Though there have not been any reports about his ghost in that region, another well-known pirate is said to appear there from time to time.

The spirit of Edward Teach, more commonly known as Blackbeard, is said to haunt the shore of Black Bird Creek at Cape Henlopen near the former town of Blackbird. He is apparently searching for treasure that was lost when his ship sank to the bottom of the creek. Both Captain Kidd and Blackbeard are also reputed to have buried treasure at Woodland Beach near Smyrna in the very early years of the nineteenth century—which would have taken no small skill on Kidd's part, since he was executed in 1701. Perhaps witnesses saw his ghost walking there along the shore.

Another pirate who lost his treasure, but under slightly different circumstances, was Theophilus Turner, a sailor who parted company with Kidd in Delaware around 1692. Turner, who had boarded a sloop heading up the bay, apparently wanted nothing more than to settle down to a quiet life in the peaceful tidewater region. Unfortunately, government officials intervened. They didn't care if Turner's raiding days were behind him—he had to pay for his crimes. Soldiers boarded the sloop while it was anchored in the Severn River, confiscated Turner's treasure, arrested the former pirate, and sent him off to England to await trial. Turner's ghost hasn't bothered to reappear to search for his gold—he knew that once the government got it, it was long gone.

James Gillian was another member of Kidd's crew, who reportedly buried a chest of gold—without the captain's knowledge—on Kelly Island in the Delaware Bay. Gillian planned to return to the island to retrieve the treasure after Kidd was executed. But the booty, which was buried between a large rock and two bare trees, was never reclaimed—at least, not in Gillian's lifetime. Residents of Kelly Island say that on warm summer nights, Gillian's ghost is sometimes seen prowling along the coast in search of the treasure.

In other tales about buccaneers, Madagascar pirates supposedly hid two large chests filled with treasure near New Castle in 1699. The preceding year, Lewes had been sacked by Pierre Canoot. And bounty was said to have been buried on Fenwick Island by the pirate Louis Guillart. Are the stories true? Perhaps one reason none of the gold has been discovered is because the landscape has changed dramatically over the years. Perhaps another, according to area residents, is that no one wants to risk wandering in the dark and coming face-to-face with the spectral presence of the Madagascar pirates or the ghosts of the bloodthirsty Canoot or Guillart.

Pirates continued to invade Delaware well into the eighteenth century. According to Hugg's article, it took an entire squadron of British soldiers to drive Don Pedro Vincent Lopez from the Delaware Bay in the late 1740s. The ghost of one man, who became regionally famous as the pirate Blueskin, is said to still hover around the dunes at Lewes. Local residents say that on bright moonlit nights, a tall spectral form in a tattered tailcoat, carrying pistols and a sword, can be seen wandering the sandy shores, perhaps searching for some of his treasure that may still be buried there.

In *Book of Pirates*, Howard Pyle recounts the story of Levi West, the stepson of Eleazar White, a respected miller who hoped that the younger man would be content to take part in the family business. Levi, restless and bored with life in the small coastal community, chose instead to run off to sea at a young age and remained away from home for almost a decade. In 1750, he returned to Lewes to collect an inheritance of 500 pounds that his stepfather had left him. When he arrived home, Levi discovered that his stepbrother Hiram had invested the money in a ship that, ironically enough, had been attacked and burned by Blueskin. Hiram never suspected that the buccaneer stood before him in his own home. Levi was able to keep his true identity secret from his family and friends, despite a jagged scar, discolored a deep blue, that marred his tanned face. He told Hiram that he would wait in Lewes until his stepbrother raised the funds that were rightfully his.

While Levi lingered, he turned his attention toward Sally Martin, the young woman that Hiram had been courting. And not long after he received his money from his stepbrother, Levi disappeared with Sally in tow. Although Sally eventually returned alone to Lewes, she told Hiram that she and Levi had married during their time together. Heartbroken, Hiram struggled to forget about Sally, his stepbrother, and everything else that had gone wrong. He soon had an opportunity for revenge, however. One summer night, he witnessed his stepbrother burying a chest filled with stolen treasure in the dunes just outside town. Shocked, Hiram watched as Levi, in true pirate tradition, killed one of his shipmates and left the body with the loot.

Hiram was so incensed by what he had seen that he captured Levi and turned him over to authorities on the *Scorpion*, a British warship that lay anchored in the harbor. Although he thought he was just bringing a murderer to justice, much to his surprise, the officers on board informed him that his stepbrother was none other than the infamous pirate Blueskin. Hiram was eligible for a substantial reward from a grateful government. But his greatest reward came after Levi was taken to England and hanged himself in his Newgate Prison cell before facing trial. Shortly afterward, Hiram married his stepbrother's widow.

Candle Magic

Although no one knows when candles first came into popular use, historical records show that they were around as early as 3000 B.C.—a time when fire itself was considered nothing less than magical. Ancient civilizations like Egypt probably used them during religious services as a way to keep evil spirits at bay. During the Middle Ages, they continued to represent spiritual purity, often being placed by the bed of someone who was dying in order to frighten off any supernatural evil. At the same time, witches reportedly used them in ceremonies to summon malicious spirits, who would wreak havoc on the neighborhood.

As a result, a variety of legends developed around candles, traveling with immigrants from their home countries to their new land. Like settlers in other portions of the country, some Delaware residents believed that a candle left burning in an empty room would cause a death in the family; one that sputtered when no breeze blew meant there would soon be a death in the family. If a candle suddenly burned low or if its flame turned blue, it signified the presence of spirits in the house.

When pirates were terrorizing the east coast of the American colonies, those hardy souls brave enough to go treasure hunting were often warned to carry lanterns containing candles that had been consecrated by the church. These were used to summon the spirits of the dead crew members who had been buried along with the pirate's treasure in order to guard it from thieves. According to Rosemary Ellen Guiley in *The Encyclopedia of Ghosts and Spirits,* "The spirits were to be summoned in the name of God and promised anything in order to help them find 'a place of untroubled rest.'" Anything—just to get them to go away and leave the loot unprotected. If the treasure hunter made any sound at all when the specter appeared, however, the treasure was said to vanish instantly. Since it was unlikely that someone could face the sudden appearance of a dead sailor without screaming or speaking, this may explain why so much pirate bounty still remains unaccounted for in Delaware.

The Eighteenth Century

OWNERSHIP OF DELAWARE (NAMED FOR THE ENGLISH LORD WHO governed Maryland) was disputed for more than a century by settlers from different countries who were determined to claim the region as their own. It was the advent of the Revolutionary War that finally drew many of the colonists together in their opposition to British rule. Only one battle—at Cooch's Bridge—occurred on Delaware soil, but more than 4,000 volunteers from the First State enlisted in the American army. They fought in all principal engagements of the war. There are nights, some Delaware residents say, when they seem to be fighting still.

Parson Thorne

The Parson Thorne Mansion in Milford, listed on the National Register of Historic Places, was inhabited in the 1730s by the town's founder, Parson Sydenham Thorne. It later became the home of the noted Delaware statesman John M. Clayton (1796–1856), who served as a state representative, senator, and secretary of state at various times in his political career. Originally a simple working-class home, the building was substantially renovated by its owners over the years, going from Colonial-style architecture to Victorian. Today an elegant red brick mansion stands in place of the original structure, overlooking the Mispillion River, where shipbuilding was once a major industry. The house and its grounds are open for public tours and are frequently used by various local groups for civic affairs.

In the years since it became publicly owned, some visitors have reported on occasion the sight of a white-haired man in Colonial-style clothing wandering about the grounds. It really should not come as a surprise, since Parson Thorne was buried in the family plot located behind the house. Though no one has been brave enough to confront the silent figure, some believe it may in fact be the mansion's former occupant, keeping an eye on the town that he helped establish so long ago.

Shades of the Green

Dover has undergone rapid expansion over the past thirty years. With a surfeit of residential and commercial development, the historic city has become Delaware's largest in area and second largest in population, growing from about sixty-two hundred people in 1950 to more than sixty thousand today. Despite these changes, Dover has retained a lot of its small-town charm, thanks in large part to its well-preserved Colonial homes and public buildings. In addition to the architecture, another Dover showplace is the tree-lined square at the center of town known simply as The Green.

William Penn created the public park in 1683. Located on South State Street across from the Kent County Courthouse and the Old State House, it has been the site of numerous dramatic events, including the reading of the Declaration of Independence to area citizens. It is said that Dover residents received the news with such delight that the ensuing celebration was highlighted by the burning of a portrait of King George of England. The Green later became the site where Delaware troops gathered to fight for the newly formed American Army. On December 7, 1787, Delaware's constitutional delegates met at the Golden Fleece Tavern, which once stood on the Green, and became the first legislators to ratify the just written Constitution of the United States.

One of the most unusual occurrences ever witnessed at the Green was the funeral held for the ghost of departed Chief Justice Samuel Chew. That's right—his ghost. Born in 1693, Chew had been appointed in 1741 as chief justice of the Three Lower Counties, as Delaware was then known, and held that office until his death three years later. Chew's restless spirit was first seen haunting The Green by a local man who was surprised to see someone standing quietly under a poplar tree late one night. According to *Delaware: A Guide to the First State,* "Upon drawing nearer, he recognized it as the late Chief Justice, standing in his favorite attitude, head bowed in deep meditation." A few nights later, the local miller recounted almost the same story with one frightening twist—the judge was beckoning him to come closer. A ripple of panic began to spread as the tale was told and retold among the townspeople.

The magistrate had not been popular in his lifetime with some of his fellow residents, who often teased him by making fun of his last name. Some clever young men would mimic a sneeze as he passed by, and others would make chewing motions. As a result, the justice apparently decided to torment not just his tormenters after his death, but any innocent bystanders that he came across as well. Invisible fingers would pull on men's coattails; women would feel a cold, menacing presence brush by them on still summer nights. His shadowy form was often seen hovering around The Green after dark, forcing many taverns and local businesses to close early because residents were too frightened to stay in town once the sun went down.

When more and more Dover residents reported Chew's presence at The Green, city officials decided they had only one course of action—to follow the time-honored English tradition of laying the justice's ghost to rest. A funeral complete with all the pomp and circumstance they could muster was organized on the specter's behalf, which at first seemed to be exactly what the ghost wanted. After they had dug a grave and "buried" Chew's spirit under the poplar tree, reports of his presence at The Green ceased for a while. But the judge apparently hadn't given up his surveillance on the city's population, as his ghost eventually returned to haunt this popular Dover square. Even today some pedestrians who stop by The Green at night have reported a chilling presence in the vicinity of the justice's "grave" and the sound of footsteps echoing from paths where no human being walks. Perhaps Mr. Chew wasn't satisfied with the last ceremony held in his honor and wants local residents to hold one that is grander still.

The Restless Spirit

Amstel House in New Castle, a town that still reverberates with Colonial charm, is one of two houses apparently haunted by the same restless spirit. A fine example of early Georgian architecture, Amstel House was built in the eighteenth century by Dr. John Finney. The unknown ghost seems less than impressed by the surroundings, however, as it also spends part of its time at the former home of the doctor's son, the David Finney Inn, just down the street. David Finney was a lawyer-soldier whose brick residence, built in 1683, today serves as a popular local restaurant. Diners can enjoy their meals and a view of the town common from the newly remodeled building. Although the present owners have not experienced anything unusual, previous occupants said that when the ghost was in residence, windows opened and closed on their own, objects moved without any visible help, and the resident pets avoided the third floor at all costs.

Cheney Clow's Rebellion

Not far from the Maryland border, just north of Everett's Corner in Kent County, lies a grassy knoll that is remembered locally as the site of Cheney Clow's Rebellion. Although nothing remains of the small wooden fort that once stood there, the now privately owned property was named in 1975 to the National Register of Historic Places because it is historically significant. What is so special about this particular patch of farmland? Area residents will tell you it is the place where Clow, a captain in the British Army, attempted to make a last stand against America at the end of the Revolutionary War.

Cheney Clow had served with the British during the French and Indian War. Unlike some of his neighbors, he saw no reason to rebel against the Crown when the Revolutionary War got under way, and for years, he felt it was his responsibility to punish them for turning away from English rule. Clow reportedly led bands of Tory marauders throughout the countryside, stealing provisions from local farmers who supported the American cause. When the farmers complained to state officials, the captain was ordered to take an oath of allegiance to prove that he was not an enemy. He refused.

In 1782, beleaguered authorities finally decided to take action against Clow, who had continued to terrorize his neighbors. A posse rode to his hillside fortress, but the men were greeted by a hail of bullets when they approached and demanded his surrender. As they exchanged heavy fire, the sheriff's men were positive that Clow had a gang of his supporters by his side. But when they stormed the house, they discovered it contained only the captain and his wounded wife.

Surrendering, Clow put on his British uniform and rode back to Dover with the posse. Later charged with treason, he convinced the jury that as an enemy officer, he was only doing his job, and as a result, he was entitled to be treated as a prisoner of war. Not everyone in the region was completely supportive of the American cause, so he gained the sympathy of some members of the jury. Clow was acquitted of treason, but he was not destined to go free. Charged with the murder of Joseph Moore, a sheriff's officer who had died in the assault on his fort, Clow was tried and convicted. But though he was sentenced to hang, it seemed that public sympathy once again lay in his quarter. More than six years passed before Gov. Thomas Collins reluctantly ordered his sentence to be carried out.

Following Clow's execution, his wife reportedly placed his body in an unmarked grave near the fortress. In recent years, archaeologists who have excavated part of the site believe that they located the spot where the captain was buried. Whether or not his body is ever found, some area residents say that Cheney Clow is still fighting for what he believed to be the right cause. Some nights when the moon is full, the sound of musket fire can still be heard ringing across the open fields from the vicinity where the hillside fort once stood.

The Ghost Who Never Was

Dr. Pierre Didier, a veteran military surgeon who emigrated to America from France, began practicing medicine in Wilmington in the early nineteenth century. His patients included many members of the du Pont family, who regularly visited his elegant brick mansion on French Street. The focus of this story is not the good doctor, however, but his house—reportedly haunted in the late eighteenth century by a sailor's ghost. Although the tale ultimately turned out not to be true, it was handed down for many years as fact.

The house, like many of the period, featured a well handily located in the yard. Legend had it that before the building was purchased and expanded by Didier, it was rented by a veteran sailor named French Kellum for his family. Kellum, who frequently spent months at sea, was feared lost around 1783 when months passed and no one received any news about the fate of his ship. Then one evening, the vessel arrived without fanfare at the Wilmington wharf, and Kellum hurried home, anxious to reassure his family of his safe return. Passing by the well, he realized that he needed to at least wash the grime of travel from his face. But when he attempted to push back the stone covering, he stumbled and fell into the well, and much to his horror, the well's heavy lid slammed shut on top of him.

For a moment, he was stunned by his fall, but he soon realized that his survival depended on his willingness to help himself. Clinging to the walls, Kellum climbed toward the surface, shouting for help. His adrenaline pumping, he found the strength to shove aside the stone lid just as his wife and the landlady appeared in the yard. As they fearfully tiptoed closer, trying to find the source of the commotion, Mrs. Kellum received a shock. The figure of her husband rose before her, dripping wet, from the depths of the well. She fell into a dead faint, because she knew that what she saw could only have been French's ghost. The fact that he was soaked through meant that her husband had been lost during his last voyage. As the landlady ran for help, Kellum attempted to revive his stricken wife, but it took him quite a while to convince her that she wasn't seeing a ghost but her flesh-and-blood husband, returned at long last from the sea.

Keeping the Faith

This is the tale of the *Faithful Steward*, a 350-ton, three-masted sailing ship that left Londonderry, Ireland, on July 9, 1785, bound for the port of Philadelphia. On board were about a hundred crew members and more than two hundred Irish immigrants, who hoped to find a better life in the New World. And with an uneventful crossing, those hopes rose higher as the vessel approached the shore.

But instead of approaching Philadelphia on schedule, the ship wound up below Cape Henlopen at the entrance to the Delaware

Bay, likely because of poor navigating. Since the treacherous sand dunes were virtually flat and thus invisible, it was too late to change course when the crew discovered their error, and the ship ran aground. Before long, it was assaulted by gale-force wind and huge waves as a storm rapidly rose off the coast. Panic spread as the elements continued to batter the ship. Because of the storm's fury, neither crew nor passengers realized that they were only about a hundred yards from shore. Soon the waves forced the *Faithful Steward* over on its side, killing and injuring many of those on board. The remaining passengers and crew spent a fear-filled night. When morning came, a number of them made several attempts to swim to shore, but the violent surf drowned so many that all efforts ceased until later, when the storm began to subside. In the end, only sixty-eight survivors were counted out of the nearly three hundred people who had been on board.

Area residents say that sometimes on stormy nights, when the surf starts to crash and the wind begins to howl, a strange silhouette can be glimpsed just about a hundred yards offshore—a wooden ship with tattered sails rocking before the wind. It seems that the ghost of the *Faithful Steward* continues to reenact the events that occurred on that fateful night, still trying vainly to reach the shore and bring her passengers safely to the New World.

Tragic Dreams

In *Delaware: A Guide to the First State,* the authors have transcribed portions of a diary kept by Aletta Clowes Clarke between 1789 and 1793, which documented her life and times. Clarke once resided at the Conwell House, a rectangular, shingled house located in east Sussex County near the Great Pocomoke Swamp. In her diary, Clarke recorded a family tragedy that apparently was foretold through the precognitive dreams of her pregnant sister.

On October 31, 1789, she wrote: "I went to see my sister. She told me of two dreams she had dreamed. In one she was dressed in white, and her company told her she did not look as if she belonged in this world. In the other her child was born, and she was to die three days afterward."

Although she did not necessarily believe what she had been told, Clarke felt it was advisable to keep a close eye on her sister's condition. At a time when childbirth was risky even among wealthier women, anything could happen. Clarke visited regularly, helping organize the household and sewing tiny garments in preparation for the infant's arrival. About six weeks later, however, on December 5, she noted in her diary: "In the morning my Brother came over and said that Sister Sally was taken with an ague, and was very sick. I went right away to see her, and found her sickness most violent. Her violent sickness brought on her labour. On Sunday the 6th at sunrise she was delivered of a son."

Worn out from nursing her sister, Clarke returned home after the baby was born. Unfortunately, the initial excitement of the baby's birth soon gave way to tragedy. December 6 would prove to be the last time she would see her sister alive. It seems that Sally's dreams, related months earlier, were destined to come true—even before the foretold three days had passed. On December 7, Clarke made one more entry in her journal about her sister. It read: "This morning . . . it pleased God to take her into His safe keeping. She was 20 years and 6 months old this day lacking 3 days."

Be Wary of Woodburn

The governor's mansion on King's Highway in Dover, known today as Woodburn, is the best-known haunted house in the state. Its long and colorful story began in 1790, when it was built by Charles Hillyard, a colonel in the Revolutionary War.

A number of spirits apparently haunt the elegant mansion, including an elderly gentleman who may be none other than Colonel Hillyard himself. Silhouettes are said to appear in the windows of empty rooms, and the house is also supposed to be visited by an unidentified young girl in a checked red dress, who has been seen wandering in the gardens. Then there is the chain-rattling ghost in the basement, who wants visitors to know that some African Americans met a terrible fate at Woodburn. The mansion was reportedly a stop on the Underground Railroad, but it is believed that some of the unfortunates who were attempting to escape north were recaptured there and ultimately returned to slavery.

Colonel Hillyard was first seen at Woodburn around 1815, when his daughter and her husband, Dr. Martin Bates, were residing there. One morning, their house guest, the Methodist preacher

Lorenzo Dow, inquired about the other person he had met on the stairs while going down to breakfast. Mrs. Bates told him no one else was staying in the house, but Mr. Dow described in specific detail the man he had just seen. When Mrs. Bates heard that the older gentleman wore a powdered wig, ruffled shirt, and knee britches, she blanched and gasped in surprise—it was an exact description of her deceased father, Col. Charles Hillyard, who had died in the house a few years earlier.

In the years that followed, other owners of the property and visitors to Woodburn also described encounters with the colonel. In the late nineteenth century, a house guest fainted after he saw the ghost of an elderly man who may have been Colonel Hillyard sitting by the fireplace. The colonel was said to have carried his love of fine wines into the afterlife. Whenever a glass of wine was left downstairs at Woodburn, residents usually discovered that he had emptied it during the night. Jeanne Tribbitt, wife of former governor Sherman W. Tribbitt, was said to regularly check the stairway for the colonel, but her efforts to lure him and some of Woodburn's other spectral residents into the open were never successful. In more recent years, Governors Pierre S. du Pont and Michael Castle permitted some students of the paranormal to conduct investigations in the mansion, but their efforts proved unsuccessful as well.

Although she may be an older presence, the young girl in the red gingham dress is commonly assumed to be a twentieth-century spirit for several reasons. The reflecting pool, which seems to be her favorite haunt, was not added to the grounds until the early twentieth century, when Woodburn was owned by Sen. Daniel Hastings (1912–18), and she was first observed playing near it in the 1940s. Perhaps she returned because construction of the pool disturbed a place that was special to her. In any event, the young spirit—who sometimes carries a candle as she strolls through the gardens—is said to enjoy teasing visitors both inside and outside the house. During Governor Castle's inauguration party in January 1985, guests complained that invisible fingers were plucking at their clothes. One woman also claimed that she had seen the child standing in a corner of the reception room during the party.

The Hanging Tree

For more than three centuries, the grounds of Woodburn were home to a tulip poplar known as "the hanging tree." Planted near the mansion in 1680, the tree frightened generations of local residents who made the mistake of walking too close to it at night. They said that if you listened closely—especially around Halloween—you could hear the sound of sorrowful moaning coming from inside the tree.

There are two versions of the story explaining the noises. According to the first, Woodburn was once a stop on the Underground Railroad. For most of the nineteenth century, the house was owned by the Cowgill family, devout Quakers who abhorred slavery. Mr. Cowgill refused to own slaves and treated blacks and whites with equal respect. Runaway slaves knew that they would find sanctuary with the Cowgills, who frequently led them to safety through a tunnel in the basement to the St. Jones River. The tunnel is gone now, but the door in the cellar remains.

Legend has it that an infamous woman named Patty Cannon and her gang made a bold attack on the house, knowing that runaway slaves were hiding there. Cannon, whose story is told at length a little later in this book, regularly kidnapped African Americans and sold them down south. One slave climbed inside the tree in a desperate effort to hide from the outlaws. But the narrow opening proved his undoing. Hampered by chains, he hung there, screaming for help. He eventually died—still trapped in the tree. Over the decades, his cries continued to echo from deep inside the poplar's trunk.

In the second version of the story, one of Cannon's raiders climbed the tree one night to scout the property, but before he could call out to his comrades, he suddenly slipped and fell. He was strangled to death when his head was caught viselike between two branches that refused to bend or break. It was said that when the moon was full, his wailing ghost could be seen struggling to get free from the tree.

When the tree was cut down in 1997, the noises stopped. Although state officials said the poplar was removed because it was growing too close to the mansion, perhaps it was because the residents were too shaken by the continuous eerie moaning to let it remain standing. Another tulip poplar was planted near the site of the first one by Governor Castle, but so far, no unusual sounds have been heard issuing from inside the new tree.

The Ghost Town and Ghost Ship

A number of small towns sprang up early on in Delaware as eager immigrants flocked to the state to take advantage of its rich supply of natural resources. Delaware's extensive forests and waterways seemed to provide everything they needed to build their homes and feed their families. Unfortunately, many of these towns did not survive through the years, often destroyed by economic difficulties, the environment, or a combination of the two.

Not much more than memories are left of Port Mahon, a fishing community that once stood east of Little Creek where the Delaware River meets the bay. Once the town consisted of a broad expanse of beach and a lighthouse, along with a few homes, fishing shacks, and piers, but today all that remains of the community are the pilings of the lighthouse, which burned in 1984. And most of the time, the pilings, along with a large portion of the Port Mahon Road, are flooded by incoming high tides.

Some area residents say, however, that the former town still holds an attraction for Capt. Joshua McCowan, whose ship can sometimes be seen off the coast on nights when the moon is full. It doesn't matter if the sea is rough or still—the captain has a good reason to try to reach land. He was in love with Sally Stout, the beautiful daughter of the governor. But before the ship could approach the shore, McCowan was murdered by one of his crew, who was jealous of their relationship. His body was hung from the bowsprit of his ship and remains there still. However, this apparently hasn't deterred him from trying to return to port to seek out his long-lost love.

The Headless Horseman of Cooch's Bridge

In 1777, Cooch's Bridge in Newark was the site where brave Delaware militiamen first flew the Stars and Stripes as they engaged the British in battle. In fact, it is documented as the only time American soldiers fought their enemies on Delaware soil. Their goal? To hold back British forces that were determined to cut off Gen. George Washington's retreat to Philadelphia. The militiamen were apparently successful, but it seems that at least one British soldier has refused, even more than two hundred years later, to give up the fight. Area residents claim that on foggy nights, you can see the ghost of a British soldier wandering the roads in search of his head, which was shot off during the Battle of Cooch's Bridge.

Locals say that part of the battle echoed around a nearby church on Welsh Tract Road that was being defended by a group of soldiers. One young patriot named Charlie Miller reportedly was caught in the line of fire and killed by a cannonball that crashed into the wall of the church. The men claimed that Charlie's head had been taken off by the cannonball, and they circulated a story that eventually unnerved the British. A headless man was said to appear on horseback in the midst of English troops, chopping off their heads as he rode past. Although no one has admitted to seeing Charlie's ghost in recent years, some say that the sound of a horse's hooves can be heard thundering down Welsh Tract Road late at night as he rides by, still ready to defend his country.

Perhaps another reason that ghosts still linger here is the prospect of finally locating a cache of gold coins said to have been buried in the region during the Revolutionary War. Legend has it that the treasure is located within the depths of the appropriately named Purgatory Woods, somewhere between Newark and Cooch's Bridge.

The Phantom Dragoon

We'll never know whether the story of Charlie Miller worked so well that it inspired the British troops to try a little psychological warfare of their own against the American soldiers. But noted American folklorist Charles M. Skinner—one of the first to collect the tales and legends told in every corner of the United States—in his classic book, *American Myths and Legends,* tells how just such a superstition almost caused a serious setback for the colonists fighting the Revolutionary War:

> The height that rises a mile or so to the south of Newark is called Iron Hill because it is rich in hematite ore but about the time of

General Howe's advance to the Brandywine it might well have won its name because of the panoply of war—the sullen guns, the flashing swords, and glistening bayonets—that appeared among the British tents perched on it. After the red coats had established camp here, the American outposts were advanced and one of the pickets was stationed at Welsh Tract Church. On his first tour of duty, the sentry was thrown into great alarm by the appearance of a figure robed from head to foot in white that rode a horse at a charging gait within ten feet of his face.

When guard was relieved the soldier begged that he might never be assigned to that post again. His nerves were strong in the presence of an enemy in the flesh—but an enemy out of the grave: Ugh! He would desert rather than encounter that shape again. His request was granted. The sentry who succeeded him was startled, in the small hours, by a rush of hoofs and the flash of a pallid form. He fired at it, and thought that he heard the sound of a mocking laugh come back.

Every night the phantom horseman made his rounds, and several times the sentinels shot at him without effect, the white horse and white rider showing no annoyance at these assaults. When it came the turn of a skeptical and unimaginative old corporal to take the night detail, he took the liberty of assuming the responsibilities of this post himself. He looked well to the priming of his musket, and at midnight withdrew out of the moonshine and waited, with his gun resting on a fence. It was not long before the beat of hoofs was heard approaching, and in spite of himself the corporal felt a thrill along his spine as a mounted figure that might have represented Death on the pale horse came into view; but he jammed his hat down, set his teeth, and sighted his flintlock with deliberation.

The rider was near, when bang went the corporal's musket, and a white form was lying in the road, a horse speeding into the distance. Scrambling over the fence, the corporal, reassured, ran to the form and turned it over: A British scout, quite dead. The daring fellow, relying on the superstitious fears of the rustics on this front, had made a nightly ride as a ghost, in order to keep the American outposts from advancing, and also to guess, from elevated points, at the strength and disposition of their troops. He wore a cuirass of steel, but that did not protect his brain from the corporal's bullet.

The Brave Chief

Skinner also related the tale of Tammany, or Tamanend, an Indian chief who once lived in Delaware. A respected leader, Tammany was one of the chiefs who approved the treaty with William Penn, which allowed his tribe to live in peace for many years with the European immigrants. As time went by, the Quakers asked the Indians to meet with them once again in Philadelphia. Although Tammany was very old by then, he decided to travel with some of the other men of his tribe to attend the meeting.

But the younger men grew impatient with Tammany's slow progress on the journey and left him behind. The chief, hampered by rheumatism, stopped to rest for a time on Prospect Hill. A young woman from his tribe stayed behind to prepare his meals, but lured by the attractions of the strange and wonderful city, she eventually left him as well. When Tammany found himself alone one night, he realized that he had outlived his usefulness and might be better off dead.

He began to add wood to the fire that warmed his tent until it became a tremendous blaze. Travelers who saw the strange glow in the night were fearful about what it meant. Was it a sign? Were evil times about to befall them? The only evil seemed to be directed at Tammany, however, and that was by his own hand. As the fire raged, the chief plunged a hunting knife into his heart and fell into the flames.

When the members of his tribe returned, they found the chief's charred body lying on Prospect Hill. They laid Tammany to rest between two trees in a place that later became the burial site for his entire family. Although many mourned his passing, some said that the chief's sacrifice proved he was a noble man, and that when he died, the flames carried his spirit upward to the happy hunting grounds. Tammany's attachment to this world apparently remained strong, however, especially to those lush forests where he had once hunted and fished. On cool autumn nights, the chief's spirit has been seen striding along the coast of Delaware, perhaps searching for the other members of his tribe.

Sunken Ships and Pirate Treasure

Like nearby New Jersey, Delaware's coast was not always a welcome sight to those traveling aboard ship in the eighteenth and nineteenth centuries. Historians estimate that more than two thousand ships have sunk in the Delaware Bay over the past three hundred years, some caused by legitimate error, but others by the "moon cussers" who patrolled the beaches, waiting for night. The moon cussers, also known as wreckers, were crews of unscrupulous men and women who lured hapless ships close to the shoreline, using decoy lights to make them think they had safe passage. They reportedly "cussed" the moon because its light sometimes prevented them from accomplishing their evil plans. When the ships did crash and sink, the moon cussers would then gather the loot that floated ashore and strip valuables from any bodies that drifted in on the tide.

Other ships were assaulted by pirates, who lay hidden in the many coves and inlets that run throughout much of the state. The ships were often robbed and burned, eventually sinking to the bottom with some treasure still on board. With the aid of modern technology, scuba divers search for the wrecks of sunken ships in the waters off the Delaware coast. But over the years, both residents and tourists have discovered they don't always have to go into the water to search for bounty. Often, the currents would free the gold from the remains of the ships and toss it onto the beach. In fact, so many coins have been retrieved this way that Delaware has even dubbed a section of shore near Rehoboth as Coin Beach because of the number of coins that continue to wash up on shore.

Some of the sunken treasure found there over the years is said to have come from the *Faithful Steward,* a passenger ship lost off the coast in 1785 that was believed to be carrying almost half a million English and copper pennies. Apparently, the coins were being sent to the United States to alleviate a shortage of hard currency. A number of coins were reportedly first found in 1931 by a Milford resident who was surf fishing along the beach. During World War II, Coast Guardsmen would sometimes find coppers lying at the water's edge. Before long, the region became known as a good spot to scavenge for treasure.

Similar fates befell both the *China Wreck* and the *deBraak,* which sank off the coast of Lewes. Reedy Island, located just a few miles south of Delaware City on the Delaware River, was also the scene of numerous shipwrecks. The fate of the *Juno,* however, remains a mystery even today. The sailing ship reportedly left San Juan, Puerto Rico, with close to a thousand passengers on October 1, 1802. As the *Juno* traveled north along the Delaware coast, gale-force winds and rough waters prevented the ship from getting close to land. After three weeks, the crew was overjoyed to finally see some help on the horizon: The *Favorite* had responded to their distress signals and was prepared to come to the *Juno*'s rescue. The ships paralleled each other for two days, but when the weather got worse, the damaged vessel disappeared from sight. To this day, the location of the *Juno* remains a mystery—one that treasure hunters are eager to solve. The ship is believed to have sunk beneath the waves with twenty-three tons of silver still on board.

Those who prefer not to dive into the bay have the option to simply visit places like Reedy Island after a storm. There, English, Dutch, and Spanish coins frequently wash in with the tide. Over the years, some treasure hunters have paid as much as $100 for maps that supposedly would guide them directly to where the treasure lies. Although the maps were usually fake, that did not discourage them from their quest to find coins, jewels, or other remnants of the past. Even today, though not everyone is lucky enough to go home with a little bit of sunken treasure, many folks have been fortunate to find a souvenir or two. The best part of treasure hunting on land is that it's perfectly legal to keep whatever is found on a public beach.

Roaming around Rockwood

The elegant forty-five-room Gothic mansion known as Rockwood, which today stands as a history museum outside of Wilmington, is one of the many haunted houses located within the state. Built in the 1850s for Joseph Shipley, a wealthy merchant banker from England, the property was last privately owned by a descendant, Nancy Sellers Hargraves. Today Rockwood is listed on the National Register of Historic Sites, and public tours are offered on a regular basis. Visitors occasionally get a little more than they bargained for when they purchase an admission ticket. Sometimes the house's former residents like to remind both visitors and staff that *they* were at Rockwood first.

Psychic investigators have reported strange noises and the appearance of mysterious balls of light, commonly called orbs, within the house, but no one has yet been able to identify who or what is their source. An employee who believed she was alone in the house during a lunch break once heard the distinctive sound of heels rushing across the second floor. A volunteer who was arranging a candlelight tour one night was surprised to see water flowing steadily down the servants' staircase. When she and her husband investigated, they discovered that the bathtub faucets in the third-floor servants' bathroom had been fully turned on, causing the overflow.

Hargraves was reportedly fearful of staying in the house alone. In volume 3 of *Welcome Inn,* author Ed Okonowicz writes that "she heard all kinds of things, all night long, walking around." Edna Blunt, a former housekeeper for the Hargraves family, later told well-known Delaware newspaper columnist Bill Frank about a cook who refused to stay at the house for more than a few days. Apparently, the woman's sleep was repeatedly disturbed by what she described as a threatening presence that lingered around her room and the servants' bathroom. Blunt said the cook told her that "it was right over her head. It was like somebody was gasping for breath." Another servant told Blunt that one day she watched in amazement as both the outer and inner back doors of the house, normally kept locked, suddenly opened and closed by themselves. Her employment at Rockwood ended shortly afterward.

Despite disturbing the lives of the former tenants, the spirits who linger at Rockwood don't seem to have ever expressed any overt signs of anger or malevolence. All the same, the servants feared them. Today, however, the museum staff does not mind sharing the house with those past residents who still walk the halls. Located on Shipley Road, Rockwood now stands on seventy-two of the three hundred original acres. The mansion and other farm buildings on the grounds are open to the public.

Fevered Spirits

Supernatural occurrences have been reported at a small Methodist cemetery outside of Dover that was abandoned many years ago. For generations, it bore silent witness to the joys and sorrows of the local population. Sorrows apparently predominated in the late eighteenth century, when, among a variety of other epidemics that were rampant at the time, an extremely fatal bilious disorder (affecting the liver) struck the region. A number of new graves were suddenly prepared for area residents who suffered a fatal bout of the disease.

It soon seemed that some of the younger victims had not reconciled themselves to the idea that their lives had been cut so tragically short. Some local residents say that a particular phenomenon can sometimes be observed around dusk on warm summer nights. As the sun goes down, tiny flickering lights—that are not fireflies—are seen hovering around the headstones of some of those youngsters who were taken by the disease. Even today the sound of childish laughter can be heard in that portion of the cemetery, perhaps resulting from an invisible game of tag while the young spirits wait for someone to finally call them home.

The Nineteenth Century

DELAWARE EXPERIENCED ITS SHARE OF PROSPERITY AS PART OF THE fledgling United States of America. Shipbuilding and shipping, agriculture, and du Pont's new gunpowder mills combined to bring new wealth to the tiny state. However, prosperity did not always bring peace and happiness to Delaware's residents. Lurid accounts of murders filled the newspapers, incursions by slave traders—who often kidnapped free blacks as well as runaway slaves—were common, and the whipping post continued to be a feature in some town squares. New legends of restless spirits were born at this time and soon were spread along with classic tales.

The Big Bang

At first glance, Hagley appears to be a quiet complex of nineteenth-century buildings on the banks of the Brandywine, northwest of Wilmington. This former home of the du Pont family is dedicated to preserving an important piece of their Delaware past. Hagley was where the now internationally famous family, with interests in banking, real estate, and other businesses, first made their fortune starting with the manufacture of gunpowder. Today tourists flock to Hagley to see what life was once like for one of Delaware's premier families.

When Eleuthère Irénée Nemours du Pont migrated from his native France to the New World, America was still a handful of colonies dominated by Great Britain. An intelligent man with an eye toward improving his finances, du Pont realized while hunting one day that there were no mills manufacturing gunpowder within the colonies. He quickly organized Hagley and imported other immigrants to work there.

The production of gunpowder was a dangerous business, however. Records maintained at the Hagley Museum and Library indicate that there were almost 300 explosions and 230 deaths at the mill between 1802 and 1921. The mills employed many Irish immigrants. According to the May 11, 1872, issue of the Dover *Delawarean,* some of them claimed over the years to have seen the ghosts of deceased relatives prior to at least two explosions. One such experience was reported by the Fisher family, who arrived at Hagley in 1847 to work for the du Ponts. A letter written in 1863 (during the Civil War) by Mrs. S. F. du Pont states: "James Fisher was in Washington at camp and awoke strangely agitated and said to his companions that he felt some disaster had occurred at home. He saw his father in working clothes with his coat off and his shirt sleeves rolled up, stoop over and kiss him. Both his father and brother were killed. Henry [du Pont] telegraphed his captain asking leave for him." James's father, Samuel, and his brother, also named Samuel, died on February 24, 1863, in an explosion at the Henry Clay powder mill.

The explosions were frequently reported in the local newspapers and in correspondence. Another letter written about a different incident that same year from William Bancroft to Edward Fulton recounted: "They had a bad powder mill explosion at the upper end of the Hagley Yards a few weeks since. There were thirteen men killed; one of them a millwright was in an engine house nearby the packing house that went off. The building was crushed down killing him instantly and severely hurt a man who was with him. A wagoner who was with his team at the door of the mill was killed and eleven more who was inside, of whom but two or three recognizable fragments were found." Many people believe that after meeting such violent death, the spirits of the victims remain behind long after their bodies are buried. Some say that the workers' cries can still be heard at night near the mill buildings, following the sound of an explosion. But the workers were not the only victims. The explosions also seriously injured or claimed the lives of some of the du Ponts. Some family members had other reasons to linger on after death, however.

One such familiar phantom who is occasionally glimpsed around the grounds of Hagley is Victorine Elizabeth du Pont, the oldest child of Eleuthère Irénée and Sophie Madeleine du Pont. Born in France on August 30, 1792, she was twenty-one when she married Ferdinand Bauduy, the son of one of her father's business partners. Unfortunately, Ferdinand died less than two months after they were married. Heartbroken, Victorine soon returned to her parents' home in Delaware. She devoted the remainder of her life to teaching Sunday school for the children of the mill workers and managing the household after her mother was injured in an explosion at the mill. Victorine died in 1861, but her trim figure, dressed in the height of French fashion, is still seen from time to time crossing the grounds, carrying a Bible in one hand and a basket of food in the other. She apparently is determined to continue her good works even in the afterlife.

The Spirit of Kensey John

Legend has it that the ghost of a woman dressed in white silk appeared to a large number of people during a house party in the 1800s at the Kensey John Homestead in New Castle. Seemingly attracted by the festivities, she was first observed standing near a baby's crib, then later sitting at the dining table with the other guests. Before anyone could question who the stranger in their midst was, she disappeared from view—perhaps satisfied that all were enjoying themselves in the home she still considered her own.

Love Hurts

Lewes is home to Fiddler's Hill, a bluff located at Rabbit's Ferry along Highway 227. Locals say that when the moon is full, the sound of fiddle music can be heard echoing wildly through the night. The story goes that in the early nineteenth century, two young men were both in love with the same beautiful woman from Sussex County. One youth, also from Sussex, resented the other, a native of Kent County. In a desperate attempt to frighten off his rival, the Sussex youth hid in a tree and ambushed the other as he approached on horseback. He waited until the rider drew closer, then began to make dreadful screeching noises with his fiddle. When the other man raced away, fearful of the demons he thought were the source of such awful sounds, the delighted fiddler started down the tree, planning to seek out the young woman. But his foot slipped, and down he plunged, dying on the spot of a broken neck. Since that time, his music has been heard at the bluff—perhaps an effort to summon his lady love from the beyond?

Or could it just be pranksters like the ones in the mid-1930s, who tormented area residents by re-creating the sounds of ghostly fiddle playing late at night. The two Lewes boys who concocted the scheme managed to scare a number of local people before their hoax was finally uncovered.

A Romantic Spirit

A pair of huge bald cypress trees once marked the entrance for carriages to the Coleman House in Lewes. According to local legend, the "bride and groom" trees were planted by Miss Margaret Coleman in honor of her upcoming marriage to a young local clergyman. The wedding apparently later took place with one minor change: Miss Margaret went to the altar with another groom. This fact did not deter the trees, at least, from enjoying a long and healthy life together.

The Epitome of Evil

She called herself Patty Cannon. No one ever knew for sure whether that was really her name—not even the men who would ultimately become her husbands. But it was a name that would become synonymous with pure evil in Delaware in the early nineteenth century.

Supposedly born in Canada as Lucretia Hanley, the daughter of a tavern maid and an English lord, Patty Cannon surfaced in Delaware in the 1800s. She ran an inn at Reliance on the southwest border of Delaware in the 1820s. In *The Entailed Hat*, a fictionalized but reportedly accurate account of her life written in 1884 by George Alfred Townsend, Cannon is described as: "a 'chunky' woman, short and thick, with a rosy skin, low but pleasing fore-head, coal-black hair [and] a pair of large black eyes, at once dar-ing, furtive, and familiar." She was physically strong, Townsend said, and "the bold tendency of Patty was to outdo men, and lead them on to audacities that they would have feared to follow in but for her courage and policy." Her first foray into crime occurred at the inn, where she was said to have murdered not just her first two husbands: More than forty unsuspecting travelers, who made the mistake of stopping by as they crossed the state line between Delaware and Maryland, also had their "last meals" there.

A rambling nineteenth-century clapboard farmhouse with a sag-ging front porch, nestled in a stand of trees, still stands on the spot. It was once recognized as Cannon's infamous inn, but researchers have since proven that the original tavern on the rural backroad was torn down long before the current structure was built. Still, it's not hard to imagine what must have happened at the site almost two hundred years ago. Past owners of the property have reported the sound of footsteps crossing otherwise empty rooms, doors slam-ming shut, and the presence of a malevolent force in different parts of the house.

Cannon apparently chose her prey for the quality or quantity of their possessions. If they carried anything that she viewed as valu-able, she'd whip out a bottle of arsenic and lace their food with a fatal dose. Since the inn was located miles from any authority, she knew she would have more than enough time to eventually dispose of the bodies, which she dumped temporarily into the basement. After enough corpses had accumulated, she would load them into her wagon and drive to an isolated field, where she left them in shallow graves. Although reports of her activities eventually filtered back to authorities in both Delaware and Maryland, no one ever seemed to be able to catch her doing anything wrong.

Murder was only part of Cannon's lifestyle, however. Working with Joe Johnson, who has been identified alternately as her third husband and her son-in-law, Cannon and a gang of outlaws recap-tured slaves and kidnapped free blacks, who were then auctioned off to the highest bidder. This heinous trade was highly profitable because neighboring Maryland was still a slave state in the 1820s. Many slaves there knew that the road to freedom lay through Delaware, so they would cross into the state via the Underground

Railroad in an attempt to make their way north. If they had the mis-fortune to be discovered by Cannon, they were recaptured and sold back down south. Free blacks who came to Delaware in search of work were often treated the same as runaway slaves, kidnapped from fields and towns, then chained in the basement of her inn (often near the moldering remains of her poisoned victims) while she contacted eager buyers.

Cannon and Johnson often carted their victims in covered wagons to Johnson's Ferry, as Woodland's Ferry was once known. They held auctions near their home on an island in the Nanticoke River for slave traders from Georgia and South Carolina. Sometimes they boarded the schooner that plied the river and traveled south with their prey to the slave markets in Georgia.

Cannon's reign of terror ended a few years after she fatally stabbed a slave trader and buried his body in a trunk on land behind her house. Although the actual year is disputed, many believed it was 1829 when a tenant farmer—who had rented some farmland from her—discovered a strange "crop" already planted there. While plowing the fields, his horse stumbled into a large hole in the ground. When he peered into the opening, he saw a large trunk and thought he had discovered hidden pirate's treasure. Pulling out the trunk and prying the lid open, the unsuspecting farmer was horrified to discover the remains of the slave trader wrapped in one of the tablecloths from Cannon's inn, with the bloody knife by his side. When he brought the murder to their attention, both Delaware and Maryland authorities realized that it was time to step up their efforts to bring Cannon to justice.

An opportunity arose when Johnson and members of their gang, after years of eluding authorities, were finally captured. In exchange for testimony against Cannon, their sentences were commuted from hanging to public whippings. Lured into the state, Cannon was arrested—news that flashed like lightning throughout western Delaware. Local residents flocked eagerly into Georgetown to see firsthand the woman who had terrorized them for so long.

But because she had lived life on her own terms, Cannon decided to approach death in the same fashion. The night before her trial, in the basement cell of the jailhouse, she slit the hem of her dress and pulled out a small bottle of arsenic, swallowing the contents and eluding authorities one last time. Patty Cannon was

buried in a paupers' field in Georgetown. But her story was far from over. Some say that Cannon's ferocious soul was unable to rest—perhaps fearful of paying the ultimate penalty for all her crimes. Both her jail cell and the graveyard became places to avoid, especially after dark, since her cold, malevolent presence reportedly haunted them both for many years. Maybe she couldn't rest because she feared that someone would find the treasure she reportedly buried on her property. About $100,000 in stolen gold is said to still be hidden somewhere near Johnson's Woods.

Although her body lay undisturbed for generations, it was one of many slated for relocation when officials decided to dig up the potter's field to enlarge the Sussex County courthouse and jail. Local legend states that as workers began to excavate the flimsy coffins, one young man decided to help himself to Cannon's skull when he discovered whose body was being moved. Despite her reputation, or maybe because of it, he hid the skull inside his jacket and took it home as a souvenir.

The skull remained lost until 1960, when the Dover Public Library received an unexpected gift. A visitor, carrying a hatbox and some documents, asked the staff if they wanted to add Cannon's skull to their collection of local artifacts. When the surprised librarians opened the box, they discovered Cannon's remains inside with documentation of her identity. A reference librarian at the library confirmed that the skull is still stored in the hatbox and is available on request for public viewing. The library plans to maintain ownership of the skull for now—until, perhaps, the ghost of the heartless Patty Cannon decides to pay a call and demand its return.

Blacksmith Magic

Many residents of Delaware in the early nineteenth century depended on the local blacksmith to ensure that their horses were shod, pots and pans were repaired, and a supply of handmade nails was always available. Some communities regarded the smith with a great deal of awe, because of his line of work. At that time, fire was considered to be a potent magical force. As a result, the blacksmith, who controlled fire, was obviously more than just an ordinary person.

According to David Pickering, "It was once common for sick children to be taken to the blacksmith so that they could be held over the anvil and thus cured of their ailment." Occasionally, the blacksmith would lightly tap the naked child who was placed on top of the anvil three times with his hammer to exorcise the illness from the body. Although such beliefs sound extremely primitive in today's modern, scientifically rational world, they were considered normal at a time when medicine consisted primarily of poultices and blood-letting with leeches.

Within Winterthur

Winterthur, near Wilmington in New Castle County, is another du Pont family home. The farmhouse originally located there was purchased in 1837 by James Antoine Bidermann, the son of a French investor in Eleuthère du Pont's gunpowder mill. He christened it Winterthur in honor of his family's estate in Switzerland. After marrying Evalina Gabrielle du Pont (another daughter of Eleuthère and Sophie du Pont), he built a new twelve-room mansion on the property for his bride.

The estate remained a du Pont family residence for generations. But in 1930, Henry Francis du Pont decided to turn Winterthur into a museum, which ultimately came to house the world's greatest collection of Americana. He also developed the gardens and farmlands around the house so that visitors could get a better idea of how settlers once lived off the land. The property opened to the public in 1951 and has continued to expand its exhibits and programs over the years into an internationally famous collection.

Renovating Winterthur into a museum remained du Pont's life work—a passion that apparently carried over after death. Anyone who has seen a tall, dark-haired man in proper Victorian ensemble around the grounds may have had an encounter with its former owner. The only survivor out of six children, du Pont found pleasure in collecting everything from stamps to kitchen furnishings. As years passed, the once shy and lonely child grew into a dedicated and well-respected scholar. Du Pont was so involved in turning the property into a museum that he actually helped clean the cases prior to its opening. It seems that he still takes pleasure in caring for the world-renowned collections housed at Winterthur, the place that remains his home.

The Wizard of Belltown

A number of African American settlements were formed in Delaware in the nineteenth century, thanks in part to a rising interest in human rights that were not predicated on a person's skin color. One such settlement was Belltown, named for Jake "Jigger" Bell, who donated land near Lewes in 1840 for the town's construction. The community soon boasted a population of about three hundred, a school, and a variety of stores, including a beauty parlor. There was also a church that was faithfully attended by area residents. But its presence did not deter them from seeking out assistance from another otherworldly source, when they felt such help was needed.

It seems the settlement was also the home of Arnsy Maull, known near and far as "the wizard of Belltown." Arnsy was considered the high priest of a cult of Devil worshippers, because how else, the locals reasoned, could he have obtained such amazing supernatural powers? He was said to be skilled at voodoo and soon attracted a large group of followers that included both blacks and whites. Did they need to make an enemy sick? Arnsy could do that. Did they want to find everlasting love? The wizard could help there too—for a price. They also credited him with the ability to conjure ghosts, frighten demons, and cure anybody of just about anything.

The wizard and his followers may have sold their souls for material gain, but he apparently lived long enough to regret what he had done. According to *Delaware: A Guide to the First State*, "Arnsy Maull on his death bed repudiated this dark religion, ordering his followers, so the story goes, to get long whips and lash the air so as to 'drive off the Devil and let the Lord in!' This they did all night, accompanying the cracks of the blacksnake whips with prayers and exhortations," Legend has it that a raging storm struck Belltown the night Maull died—supposedly sent by an angry Satan, who had arrived too late to carry the wizard's soul to Hell. As a result, some Belltown residents even today tend to stay close to home when bad weather arrives. They reportedly prefer not to be out just in case the Devil is on the prowl, still angry enough to take home a substitute for Arnsy Maull.

The Doomsday Cult

Religious fanatics have populated history as long as there has been human civilization. Extremists among them have promoted the idea of a doomsday—that humanity will meet a violent end because it has collectively sinned against the supreme being. In modern times, people shudder over the stories of radicals like Jim Jones and David Koresh, whose followers died because of their beliefs, but such men are just contemporary versions of an old, old story.

In the first half of the nineteenth century in America, there was an upsurge of interest in religion that did not always lead the public to established houses of worship. One such sect that was born during the Great Awakening was the Millerites, led by William Miller, a farmer from northern New York. After studying the Bible at length, Miller decided that humanity was damned and began his own doomsday cult. He soon attracted a following as he preached throughout the region that the world would be destroyed by fire on April 3, 1833. When his prediction didn't come to pass, Miller immediate adjusted the date to 1843—sufficient time to allow the members of his growing flock to get their affairs in order.

In the years that followed his first prediction, more than fifty thousand people gathered at various locations to hear him prophesy the coming of the hellfire that humanity had brought upon itself. One of those places was the Old Brandywine Academy, an eighteenth-century schoolhouse that was later converted into a meeting hall. The farmer-turned-preacher received additional public attention after his prophecies were published in the *New York Herald*. But when a comet appeared in the sky in March 1843, a number of his followers didn't wait to see if Miller's prediction would come true. With implicit trust in their leader, they killed first their families, then themselves. Others waited, but when they gathered on a hill behind Miller's house the following month, they were left disappointed once again.

On April 4, the date was shifted to July 7. On July 8, Miller moved the date to March 21 of the following year. Frustrated with their leader's apparent inability to provide them with a true date for the apocalypse, the Millerites began to disband. Not many of them chose to believe him when the preacher announced that October 22, 1844, was *it*—the absolute, certain end of the world. The majority of Miller's flock dispersed, although a fragment of the group went on the form the Seventh Day Adventists. Today the Old Brandywine Academy offers visitors a glimpse of the past where Miller and his followers once congregated. The two-story stone building has been converted into a museum that is operated by the Daughters of the American Revolution.

Poe's Curse

Did noted American author Edgar Allan Poe once lay a curse on the entire state of Delaware? It is said that after being thrown out of a Wilmington pub, Poe declared, "May all who are born here, die here, and may all who come here never leave."

Newark residents don't know about the rest of the state, but Poe apparently left his mark on the Deer Park Inn and Tavern on Main Street, a popular watering hole since the early nineteenth century. The tragic figure whose writings inspired generations of authors was known to wander from city to city, often in search of employment or inspiration for his work. Poe was said to have composed his poem "The Raven" at the inn, where slave traders met to sell their human wares. Over the years, inn patrons have reported strange sounds coming from the empty stairwells and the front doors swinging open as though letting through an invisible patron. Perhaps it is Poe's ghost, who reportedly died in 1849 at age forty, a victim of chronic alcoholism, still seeking sanctuary in one of the taverns where he felt most at home.

The Moors of Cheswold

Although the community of Cheswold lies just northwest of Dover, it stands worlds apart from that bustling city. Cheswold traces its roots to 1856, when the tiny town became a stop on the newly built Delaware Railroad. It soon grew into a shipping hub, where agricultural products moved through on their way to larger cities. Before long, the local economy became so solid that Cheswold boasted five stores and all the other amenities that made it a good place to raise a family.

Unfortunately, it eventually became—like so many similar towns—a victim of shifting economic priorities. The railroad lines disappeared and, with them, a number of residents who once called Cheswold home. In recent years, the census records a population of less than three hundred people. But even though Cheswold is no longer the bustling community it was in the nineteenth century, one group has remained: the people who refer to themselves as Moors. Their history includes a variety of romantic explanations for their mixed racial heritage.

According to some local residents, the Moors' ancestors were Spanish and African privateers who ultimately became shipwrecked on the Delaware coast. The stranded sailors, who may also have been French or Moorish, soon made a home for themselves among the Native American population that resided there at the time. They intermarried with the Indians and started the line that eventually became known as the Moors.

Another local legend says that the Moors of Cheswold are descended from a wealthy Irish woman named Requa, or possibly a Spanish lady from Sussex County, and a Moorish chief who had come to American shores. He may have been part of a group of Spanish Moors who reportedly founded a colony on Tangiers Island along the Atlantic coast before the start of the Revolutionary War. In another version of the story, the chief was actually the wealthy woman's slave, who turned out to have been a captive prince. After the couple wed, they had numerous children, who wound up marrying into the region's Native American population. In yet another variation of this tale, the wealthy woman purchased seven Moorish couples, whose children intermarried with the local Indians.

In the 1943 book *Delaware's Forgotten Folk*, C. A. Weslager states that about five hundred local residents who considered themselves Moors lived at that time in Sussex County. Although they had long been associated with Cheswold, according to Weslager there was some indication that they originally farmed in an isolated enclave along Woodland Beach. The Moors apparently were forced farther inland in the nineteenth century, when violent storms caused flooding to their homesteads, settling in their current home. Since no one has yet been able to provide a more scientific explanation regarding the origin of the unique group, the legends of the Cheswold Moors linger on.

Dr. Stout

Henry Vinal Storms Stout was born in 1855 in Keyport, New Jersey, but spent some of his most important moments in Delaware, which became his adopted state at a very young age. After attending public school in Dover, he eventually went on to study medicine at Hahnemann Medical College in Philadelphia. In 1898, he returned to Delaware and moved to Cheswold, where he practiced medicine for three years. Unlike many of his contemporaries, Dr. Stout apparently was not impressed by the "modern science" of the period. It seems that he had learned early on the value of homeopathic medicine and often used natural herbal cures to treat his patients. Obviously sympathetic, he understood that many local residents preferred such home remedies to anything the fledgling scientific medical community had to offer.

In addition to belonging to the Masons, Dr. Stout was a member of numerous homeopathic medical societies in Delaware, New Jersey, and Pennsylvania. Some Cheswold residents say that on warm summer nights, a buggy is seen standing just on the edge of the forest outside town, where he used to search for the herbs that he made into medications. A light can sometimes be seen flickering through the trees as though the good doctor will not rest until he finds just the right specific remedy—even though his patients have long been beyond his help.

Cursed Ground

Another local story has it that a lazy man who had rented a few acres of ground near Cheswold was evicted by his landlord when his year's lease was up. Angry over being uprooted from his comfortable life, the tenant swore to get even with the owner as he left the property. Although no one paid much attention to his threats at the time, local residents had occasion to recall the man's words before long, when the new tenants seemed to become the victims of a curse he had laid upon the property. Before the next year was out, the husband was declared insane and placed in an asylum, and his wife soon became paralyzed and was rendered physically helpless.

Miss Mary Ann

Mary Ann was the oldest of thirteen children born to Abraham and Harriet Shadd, an African American couple living in Wilmington at a time when Delaware forbade black residents from receiving any form of education. Determined to ensure a better life for their children, the Shadds moved to West Chester, Pennsylvania, and placed ten-year-old Mary Ann in a Quaker boarding school. She learned to be socially conscious at an early age, because her father was a supporter of abolition and a conductor on the Underground Railroad. In addition to his teachings, Mary Ann was further inspired by the Quaker doctrine she learned at school and became outspoken and proactive about her beliefs.

By age sixteen, she returned to Wilmington to open her own private school for African Americans. Unfortunately, the Shadd family found it necessary to move to Canada when the U.S. government passed the Fugitive Slave Law in 1850, which stated that anyone suspected of being a runaway slave could be arrested and sold down south, placing all blacks at risk. Undeterred by the racism of her homeland, Mary Ann wrote a pamphlet and later published the *Provincial Freeman*, a weekly newspaper outlining opportunities for blacks north of the American border. She eventually became an advocate of abolition, denouncing before both blacks and whites the evils of slavery.

In 1856, she married Thomas F. Cary of Toronto and opened another school that promised parents there would be no discrimination based on skin color. When the Civil War erupted, Mary Ann returned to the United States and became an Army recruiting officer for African American volunteers in Indiana. Widowed during the war, she later moved to Washington, D.C., where in 1883 she became the second black woman in the country to earn a law degree from Howard University. She continued to teach and lecture and also became an advocate of the women's suffrage movement. Mary Ann died of cancer in 1893, but some Wilmington residents say that over the years, her spirit has been seen hovering around the city, especially in lower-income areas. Perhaps she remains determined to keep fighting for civil rights even after death.

"God Help Us All"

Delaware's ship-building industry thrived in the nineteenth century, producing vessels of all shapes and sizes for both private and commercial use. Many early coastal communities were bounded by forests, where wood was readily available for construction. One such town was Milton, located on the banks of the Broadkill Creek just north of Georgetown. Founded in 1672 by English immigrants, it was known by a number of different names in the years that followed. In 1807, the community was renamed in honor of John Milton, the English poet. Today the tiny town boasts an assortment of restored Colonial and Victorian homes. Strolling down the tree-lined streets, you could easily turn the clock back about 150 years to the time when the town's ship-building industry was at its height.

In 1863, the master carpenters at the shipyards produced their masterpiece, the *Mary G. Farr,* one of the largest vessels ever built at Milton. In *Tales of Delaware,* Roger Martin describes the two-masted schooner as more than 129 feet long and weighing 330 tons. It sailed for more than twenty years, carrying fresh produce to cities all along the East Coast of the United States. Captained by Milton resident John Conwell, who was also a part owner, the *Farr* was attempting a dangerous journey home during the winter of 1886 when it ran into a fierce storm off the coast of New Jersey.

The ship was eventually tossed closer to the Delaware shore by the crashing waves, but the crew at the nearest lifesaving station was unable to help because of the violent weather. The storm eventually cleared, but Martin says that "at daybreak the beach was strewn with charred and broken wreckage with no signs of life." Everything was lost—the crew, the cargo, and the ship itself. During an investigation, it was discovered that not one but two fires may have broken out aboard the *Farr.* When the crew attempted to escape the burning ship on a lifeboat, they were tossed like rag dolls into the raging surf.

Although it was not the first ship or the last to be lost along the Delaware coast, more evidence about the *Mary G. Farr*'s fate surfaced almost fifty years later, in the early days of Prohibition. During a raid in Townsend's Inlet, New Jersey, a local sheriff discovered a bottle that appeared to hold something besides "white lightning." According to Martin, when the sheriff broke open the bottle, "inside was a strip from an oilskin slicker upon which was scribbled: 'Aboard the *Mary G. Farr*—Fire gaining in hold. Can no longer ride out gale. About to take to long boat. God help us all.'"

Fortress of Fear

Pea Patch Island is an innocent-sounding name for a place that would eventually become the location where thousands of Confederate prisoners died during the Civil War. And the violence of their deaths apparently has caused many of those restless spirits to linger, trapped in the very place they so desperately tried to escape.

The small island located off the shore of Delaware City was not even known to exist until the early nineteenth century, when a barge reportedly carrying fresh peas ran aground and spilled its cargo onto the sandy shore. Dubbed Pea Patch as a result of the accident, the island soon came to the attention of government officials, who saw the advantage of using it for military purposes.

Around 1813, earthworks were constructed on Pea Patch Island, and six years later, a brick fortress was added to the site. Known as Fort Delaware, the facility undoubtedly was built to safeguard the coast from a British invasion. But it wasn't British soldiers but Confederate ones who eventually were imprisoned there—men who ultimately christened the place the "Fort Delaware Death Pen."

The first prisoners arrived in 1862, after the Battle of Kernstown. Upon their arrival, 250 Confederate soldiers were housed in hastily constructed wooden barracks, which had the capacity to hold about 2,000 prisoners. That may have been sufficient space at first, but any additional shelter that was thrown up never managed to keep pace with the growing prison population. Within the year, 12,500 prisoners were transferred to the already overcrowded fort after the Battle of Gettysburg.

Diseases such as malaria and typhoid fever ran rampant through the fort, killing more than 2,700 Confederate soldiers. Many of their ghosts supposedly haunt both the small cemetery on the island and the cemetery at nearby Finn's Point, New Jersey, where some of the soldiers' bodies were also buried. During the war, about 300 prisoners made daring escape attempts from Fort Delaware. Though some were successful, reaching sanctuary with sympathetic family members and friends on shore, a number of them were not. And it seems that their shades still linger on the island. Visitors have reported seeing pale figures in uniform peering out at them through the holes in the walls through which the cannons were fired.

One tragic figure was a clever Confederate drummer boy who tried to fool his captors by faking his own death. With the help of some of his fellow prisoners, he thought he would make his escape once his coffin was taken to shore for burial at Finn's Point. Unfortunately, his plan proved fatal when the men who were scheduled to "bury" him were transferred to other duties. Their unsuspecting replacements never realized that the boy was still alive when they placed his flimsy coffin in the ground. His spirit is often reported seen hovering outside the fort.

The restless spirit of Confederate General James Archer, one of the men taken prisoner following the Battle of Gettysburg, is also said to haunt Fort Delaware. After his plans for a mass escape failed, Archer was placed for weeks in solitary confinement. His quarters were the dank powder magazine, where he acquired an illness that ultimately proved fatal. The general's cold, ghostly presence is said to still wander within the dark cell, moaning and rattling his chains.

Fort Delaware's ghosts are not limited to the island. Visitors have reported seeing the hands of two men in the waters off the coast, believed to be those of Confederate soldiers who vainly attempted to swim the river to freedom. As the guards watched, the two exhausted prisoners sank beneath the water, their hands stretched skyward in one last desperate signal for help.

Fort Delaware was later used by the military for coastal defense during World War I and II. A state-owned park since 1951, the site is open to the public and offers ghost tours around Halloween. Further visitor information can be found at www.destateparks.com/fdsp/fdsp.htm.

Between Heaven and Hell

Unusual place names crop up throughout the United States, but only Delaware seems to lay claim to a Little Hell, once located on U.S. Route 113 between Dover and Milford. Settled around 1870, the community consisted primarily of African Americans who were brought to the region by Jonathan Willis, a fruit grower who needed workers on his farm. The town was located directly across from Little Heaven, a settlement of Irish immigrant fruit farm workers established at about the same time by Jehu Reed. Little Heaven supposedly got its name because conditions there were such an improvement over what the immigrants had known in their homeland. Although the towns were hardly divine or hellish, the poetic imagery of the names was complemented by that given to the small brook that ran between the two communities: the River Styx. Some of the original cabins built by Reed to house his workers remain standing, along with a fruit stand, marking the location of Little Heaven, but all that remains on the site of Little Hell is a weeping willow.

The Terrible Twosome of Fox Lodge

The history of civilization has always been marred by outrageous acts of cruelty, either on a collective or an individual basis. In earlier times, it was relatively simple for villains to disappear from one place and reappear in another. All they had to do then was rechristen themselves with new names and obtain new occupations, and chances were good that they could live virtually undetected for the remainder of their lives. Fingerprinting, and DNA testing, and other scientific forms of identification simply didn't exist then to foil the plans of criminals.

Some speculation exists about a mysterious couple who settled in New Castle in 1855. Little is known about Allan Vorhees Lesley and his wife, Jane, either prior to their arrival in Delaware or during their days at Fox Lodge, the home they built at Lesley Manor. Listed since 1994 on the National Register of Historic Sites, this Gothic Revival mansion is painted pale yellow and trimmed with soft maroon gingerbread. In recent years, it has been turned into a popular bed-and-breakfast.

But not every guest is traveling through. The ghosts of both Allan and Jane Lesley have been seen in different rooms throughout the house by both owners and visitors. According to the Classes, the current owners of the property, the pale figure of a woman is periodically seen looking through the window at the foot of the servants' staircase at the back of the house. An elderly man dressed in all-white, nineteenth-century clothing frequents the second-floor sitting room. Lesley, who practiced medicine, was said to have treated patients in that room.

But could the Lesleys, in fact, have been none other than the notorious LaLauries, a couple who barely escaped New Orleans with their lives when the truth about their monstrous personalities emerged? Louis and Delphine LaLaurie became the toast of New Orleans in the 1830s, wining and dining friends at their sumptuous mansion, which in 2003 still stood at the heart of the French Quarter. But when a mysterious fire broke out one night during a dinner party, their guests were shocked to discover a number of terrified slaves chained in a secret room, where the couple had been torturing them—in some cases for years. Local residents of New Orleans became so enraged when they discovered what had happened in their midst that they attacked the house, ready to lynch both Louis and Delphine. The couple escaped, however, slipping away in the confusion to an unknown destination. For a time, they were reported to have been seen in Paris, in New York, and occasionally out west. Is it possible that they simply traveled east, eventually settling in the quiet community of New Castle?

Allan Lesley, like Louis LaLaurie, was a doctor. And the current owners of Fox Lodge discovered soon after they purchased the house that it contained several hidden chambers. While studying the original blueprints of the house one day, Elaine Class discovered a notation by the builder that he had incorporated two hidden rooms into the design. The first was located above the ceiling of a second-floor bedroom closet, the second behind a wall in the butler's pantry. But the hidden rooms weren't the lodge's only secret. The Classes also discovered a door in the basement that opened to a collapsed tunnel that once led directly to a small lake. The Lesleys reportedly used the tunnel to go rowing in the summer—or could it have been to dispose of any incriminating remains in a convenient body of water?

The idea may not be so far-fetched. After Jane died in 1870, Allan remained at Fox Lodge until his death in 1888. The couple had no children, and the house remained vacant until it was purchased in 1903 by the Deemer family. While cleaning the house, the new owners made a disturbing discovery: a pile of human bones in a dark corner that proved to be the chained-together remains of an unknown man and woman. If they—and others like them—had died at the hands of the Lesleys, that might explain why the couple still remains in residence at Fox Lodge.

The Grand Opera House

Wilmington's Grand Opera House is a beautifully restored, four-story, white wedding cake of a building on Market Street that has been returned to the grandeur of its early years. Built in 1871 under the auspices of the Masons, the Victorian-era opera house features crystal chandeliers, trompe l'oeil panels, stenciling, and gold leaf accents, as well as an eleven-hundred-seat theater. The theater was popular for generations, featuring appearances by nationally known stars such as Edwin Booth, Ethel Barrymore, and George M. Cohan. Today the opera house remains a major attraction in the city of Wilmington, annually hosting theater performances and concerts ranging from country to classical.

But some nights, it is said, the show goes on even after the last curtain call. The salons, those reception rooms where ladies and gentlemen in evening dress gathered over the years to drink champagne during intermission, whisper back to life after the audience and players have gone home. Soft laughter, the tinkling of crystal champagne flutes, and the sounds of conversation can be heard echoing through the halls as the ghostly audience enjoys yet another night at the opera house, knowing that—for them—the show will always continue to go on.

Picture Perfect

Don't be alarmed if you happen to see a balding man with a gray handlebar mustache and piercing eyes strolling through the hallways of the Darley Manor Inn in Claymont. If he's dressed in proper Victorian fashion, you may have just met Felix O. C. Darley, a world-renowned illustrator born in 1822 in Philadelphia to actor parents. In addition to providing highly detailed drawings for the works of Edgar Allan Poe, Darley also illustrated books for other noted authors, including Nathaniel Hawthorne, Charles Dickens, and Washington Irving.

Darley bought the late-eighteenth-century house in 1850 and christened it the Wren's Nest. He lived there until his death in 1888. Although it was abandoned for many years, the house was converted in 1993 into the Darley Manor Inn, a popular bed-and-breakfast stop for travelers. And it also seems to remain popular with the artist, who apparently still considers it his home.

Garfield's Ghost

According to a report filed with Paranormal News, a website specializing in tales of the supernatural and more, the following article appeared in the October 6, 1881, edition of the Wilmington *Morning News:*

> Peninsula people have been seeing ghosts and supernatural objects with alarming frequency during the last three weeks. [In Sussex County,] William West, a farmer living near Georgetown saw almost an identical appearance of the vision seen [that same week in Maryland]. He saw bands of soldiers of great size in dazzling uniforms, their muskets quivering and shimmering in the pale weird light that seemed to be everywhere, marching with military precision and presenting arms to the sound of unheard commands. The vision was startling and lasted long enough to be seen by several of his neighbors. A man named Coverdale, who was driving through the country on a lonely road, to his astonishment saw the same band of soldiers. Many people living near Laurel saw the same extraordinary phenomenon at the same time. They felt they saw in the midst of the soldiers, conspicuous by reason of his size and commanding presence, the hero and martyred President Garfield. These strange and supernatural appearances were seen by many people, among them the superstitious who have circulated the belief that the world will speedily come to an end.

The supernatural phenomenon apparently occurred shortly after James A. Garfield, the twentieth president of the United States, died on September 19, 1881. Garfield had been shot on July 2 by Charles J. Guiteau, a frustrated political office seeker. The wounded president lingered for months but eventually succumbed to blood poisoning after doctors used nonsterile methods while attempting to treat his wounds.

Deadly Storms

Lewes was struck by a series of violent storms in the late 1880s that cost the lives of many residents and a number of ships. The Blizzard of '88 occurred that March, with fierce snowstorms and gale-force winds wrecking countless vessels. The town's four-year-old lifesaving station soon proved its worth, as the crew rescued hundreds of sailors from the frigid waters. They also swung into action the following year, when the town was hit by the Great Storm of 1889. It was during that tumult that the pilot boat *Enoch Turley* disappeared with five pilots and five crew members on board. Some Lewes residents note that there are nights when the pale outline of the sturdy ship can sometimes be seen out on the bay, being tossed on the waves like a child's toy even when the weather is clear, still trying to find its way to port.

A Poisonous Affair

In the late nineteenth century, one Dover couple discovered that wealth and social position were inadequate protection against heartache. They became involved in a nationwide scandal after their daughter was callously murdered by her husband's jealous lover.

John Brown Pennington served two terms as a U.S. congressman from Delaware. His professional success was complemented by an idyllic family life; together with his wife, Rebecca, Pennington raised two daughters and two sons in Dover. Little did he realize, however, that both his personal and professional life would ultimately be damaged by something as innocent as the marriage of his youngest daughter.

In 1891, Elizabeth Pennington, known to her family as Mary, married John P. Dunning, a young reporter for the Associated Press. The newlyweds lived in Delaware for four years, until John was reassigned to serve as chief of the San Francisco news bureau. At first thrilled at the idea of moving to the "Wild West," Elizabeth soon became homesick. Sheltered and naïve as she was, it was difficult for her to adjust to the Barbary Coast's freewheeling, and frequently questionable, moral standards.

When their first child, Mary, was born, Elizabeth focused on her role as a young wife and mother. The year after their daughter's birth, however, Elizabeth discovered that her husband was having an illicit affair with forty-one-year-old Cordelia Botkin, who had deserted her own husband and country life for the glamour of San

Francisco. Cordelia shared nearby hotel rooms with her son, Beverly, and his mistress, Louise Seeley.

Thanks to Cordelia's influence, John began drinking and gambling heavily at the racetrack. Before long, he was demoted and ultimately fired amid rumors that he had embezzled funds from the office. Shocked by his behavior, Elizabeth returned to her family in Dover to try to avoid a scandal. Unfortunately, her departure left John free to move in with Cordelia and share her bohemian lifestyle full-time.

Years passed. John was eventually sent on assignment to Cuba and Puerto Rico to cover the Spanish American War. While he was away, Elizabeth received a series of anonymous letters detailing her husband's affair. The letters, sent by Cordelia, may have been an attempt to get John's wife to file for divorce. When her efforts failed, she then forwarded Elizabeth a box of chocolates and a note declaring, "With love to yourself and baby. Mrs. C." Elizabeth, who had a well-known sweet tooth, readily accepted the gift, assuming that the candy had come from Mrs. Corbally, a family friend.

It was a warm summer night that August 9, 1898. After their meal, Elizabeth and her family retired to the front porch, where she passed around the box of chocolates. By the following day, anyone who had eaten the filled bonbons became violently ill. Although most of the family recovered quickly, Elizabeth and her older sister, Ida Deane, died painfully a few days later. At first the family doctor attributed their illness to cholera morbus, a generic term used to describe a variety of stomach ailments in those days. He eventually realized, however, that they had been the victims of arsenic poisoning. Elizabeth's grieving family sent for John Dunning, who arrived the following week. When he saw the note attached to the chocolates, John declared that the gift could only have come from Cordelia.

Cordelia Botkin was arrested, and the case soon became the tabloid sensation of the day. Details about her freewheeling lifestyle were scrupulously recorded in William Randolph Hearst's *San Francisco Examiner* and relayed nationwide. After the trial began on December 6, 1898, the entire country read that the candy and arsenic had both been purchased in San Francisco stores by a woman who bore a suspicious resemblance to Cordelia. With distraught members of the Pennington family looking on, the prosecution presented handwriting analyses and chemical testing as part of its case. Although the defendant eventually presented credible alibis during her testimony, the jury convicted her after just four hours' deliberation.

The verdict was not a complete victory for the prosecution, however. A first-degree murder conviction normally would have resulted in the death penalty. But because the court was reluctant to order such punishment for a woman, Cordelia was sentenced to life imprisonment in San Quentin. She eventually died of what was diagnosed as softening of the brain, due to melancholy, on March 7, 1910.

Although the Pennington house was torn down years ago, Dover residents say that on warm summer nights, the faint image of a woman in Victorian dress can be seen hovering around the neighborhood where her family home once stood. She apparently is reluctant to leave the one place on earth where she had been truly happy during her lifetime.

Who Killed Katie Dugan?

Katie Dugan was another young Delaware resident whose life was tragically cut short by murder. But to this day, no one knows who killed her, which is probably why her spirit still cannot find rest.

The year was 1892, and Wilmington was already a bustling city. Although not wealthy, the Dugan family apparently led a comfortable enough existence in their Lancaster Avenue home. In *Bill Frank's Delaware,* the author tells how, one cool October night, the Dugans' seventeen-year-old daughter, Katie, left the house in her best dress. Although her parents did not know it, she was off to meet a boyfriend. When she failed to return home at the expected time, her parents, together with some friends and neighbors, organized a search that abruptly ended with a fatal discovery the following day.

That was when a local businessman found the body of a young woman who had been brutally beaten, then stabbed, beneath a persimmon tree near a downtown hospital. It was Katie. Although her boyfriend was eventually brought in for questioning, he had an alibi for that night, so the authorities had no choice but to release him. "The Ballad of Katie Dugan," written a few months after her death by Sam Richardson, became a popular area song that related a colorful version of what happened on that fateful night. As Wilmington police continued their investigation, they were hounded by city residents who were scandalized by the fact that poor Katie's killer had not yet been caught. According to Frank, one interesting tidbit of information that did come to light during the search for the murderer was the fact that Katie had been pregnant.

A $200 reward was offered, but it wasn't until two years later that there was another apparent break in the case. A Wilmington businessman who had previously employed Katie as a maid was arrested and charged with the heinous crime. A New Castle County grand jury eventually found, however, that there was not enough evidence against him for a trial, so he was ultimately released. A private detective who worked with police on the case hinted for years afterward that he had a good idea as to who was responsible for Katie's death. But he took that person's name with him when he died in 1933.

To this day, no further evidence has been forthcoming. And that is why, some Wilmington residents say, they have seen Katie Dugan, in her best dress, walking down Lancaster Avenue on cool October nights, headed unsuspectingly toward her fatal meeting. It seems that she remains destined to continue taking that final stroll, because her killer has never been found.

The Twentieth Century

D**UE TO THE GROWING NUMBER OF COMPANY HEADQUARTERS THAT MADE** their home here, Delaware was eventually nicknamed "the Corporate State." But a number of picturesque small towns with populations in the hundreds, struggled to maintain their identities while Delaware's major cities grew at a sometimes alarming rate. Increased environmental and historic preservation efforts resulted in the conservation of endangered lands and significant structures, reminding both residents and visitors of the importance of protecting the First State's fragile ecosystem as well as its past. Also conserved are more tales of regional residents, who sometimes seem to have difficulty moving on to the afterlife.

Ardent for Arden

In 1900, a network of villages collectively known today as the Ardens was born in Delaware. The Ardens, listed on the National Register of Historic Places, is the country's only Utopian enclave to last longer than a century. The principals on which they were founded violated just about every popular standard of living in America at the time, but the residents cared little about what others thought. The "radicals" who inhabited the community shared a belief in commune-style living and the single-tax principle promoted by journalist Henry

George. His idea was that a single tax should be charged on land, with no tax whatsoever on wages or interest. Ardenites also believed that government was unnecessary, because people would ultimately handle their civic responsibilities. In Arden, one of many such communities founded during this period, the residents apparently prided themselves on being socially conscious—a feeling that, for one woman in particular, didn't seem to pass with death.

One of the town's better-known inhabitants was Sinclair Lewis, author of *The Jungle,* a disturbing book about working conditions in Chicago's meat-packing industry. Prior to this book's publication, Lewis wrote many articles about child labor in America, attempting to raise the public's awareness about working conditions for the young. He was joined in this campaign by another Arden resident who was equally passionate about the rights of the working class.

Ella Reeve Bloor would be recognized nationwide in her lifetime as "the Queen of Communism," at a time when communism spread among the working class in response to the overtly greedy capitalist spirit that was rampant in America. According to Bloor's biography, *We Are Many,* one of her first civic tasks when she moved to the community was to assist Lewis with his research. She took him to Bridgeton, New Jersey, so that he could observe conditions in the glass factories there firsthand. Bloor, who had tried domestic life as a young wife and mother, discovered early on that she was meant to support public causes. She was active in the women's suffrage movement, and as a union representative, she often found herself on the front lines of strikes.

In the years that followed, Arden continued to draw creative people from all fields. It has been home to performers, such as Anthony Perkins and Jack Klugman, as well as the popular author and newspaper columnist Bill Frank. Today Arden residents continue to uphold the beliefs of their founders and former residents, including Lewis and Bloor. Many current residents describe themselves as free thinkers who probably would have felt right at home in the bucolic community more than a hundred years ago. That's probably why Bloor, who moved constantly during her lifetime, not only maintained fond memories of the time she spent in Arden, but also seems to have found her way back. Since her death in 1951, some local residents have noticed a pale, slim figure in the vicinity where a little red house (which may have once been known as

Assembly Place) still stands, occupied in fact by her descendants. Apparently Bloor likes the idea of staying close to a place that still strongly reflects the values she maintained during her lifetime.

The Forest Spirit

Redden, Delaware's largest state forest, annually draws thousands of visitors who enjoy hiking, canoeing, and fishing in the verdant woods. A portion of the Pennsylvania Railroad once crossed the region. The station house, in an isolated section of the forest, eventually was converted into a hunting lodge when the line closed down. The building later became the ranger's residence, but it seems that the ranger was not the only person to be quartered there.

In the early 1900s, a young woman reportedly died in the house under mysterious circumstances, and her spirit is believed to have hovered there ever since. Over the years, visitors to the building have reported the presence of "cold spots," areas of frigid temperature indicating a supernatural presence, as well as strange sounds and eerie voices coming from empty rooms on the second floor. In addition, lights and appliances suddenly turned themselves off and on. Although the young woman's death is documented, no one knows anything further about who she was or how or why she died.

Ghostly Writing

The phenomenon of automatic writing is familiar to many people who have studied the supernatural. Essentially, a person who goes into a receptive, trancelike state then develops the ability to scrawl messages from the spirit world. One unique case that reportedly occurred in Delaware in the early years of the twentieth century involved a du Pont descendant, who not only communicated with the dead through writing, but also dabbled in spectral photography.

Marguerite du Pont Lee was a well-known society matron with a strong interest in such diverse areas as the paranormal and women's rights. The author of *Woman's Position in the Episcopal Church,* she later wrote *Virginia Ghosts,* one of the first collections of folktales in the United States. Lee began experimenting with automatic writing following the death of a close personal friend, Episcopal minister Kemper Bocock, in 1904. According to Lee, the writings from Bocock instructed her to try her hand at photography—with some highly unusual results. When she developed the pictures she had taken of Bocock's portrait placed in a chair, Lee reportedly saw it surrounded by orbs and ghostly faces, including that of her deceased friend.

In an effort to improve communication with Bocock, Lee began to have her own picture taken by a "spirit photographer" named William M. Keeler. The minister soon began to appear in almost every photograph, but there was one noticeable problem. His body never seemed to be consistently proportioned from one shot to the next. Lee eventually asked psychic investigator Walter Prince to examine the more than four thousand photographs that Keeler had taken and was alarmed to learn that he believed they had all been faked. Unfortunately, Lee's photographs have disappeared from public view, so it is impossible to say if her own efforts to contact the "other side" and actually reach the departed Kemper Bocock were successful.

Seaside Spirits

Woodland Beach in Kent County is not so wooded now, but in the early 1900s, visitors flocked to the resort town to enjoy a variety of attractions developed by James Mott. The enterprising entrepreneur drew crowds to the shore town by building a boardwalk there, complete with carnival rides, concession stands, and a dance hall. Apparently, many of these visitors so enjoyed the novelty of strolling wooden planks along the waterside, enjoying unique treats, games, and dancing, that they linger still along the coast. The boardwalk is long gone now, except for a handful of pilings that stretch up by the shore. But local residents say that when the moon is full, ghostly figures in Victorian costume can be seen flitting across the water where the boardwalk once stood, perhaps waiting for the ferry that once ran to and from Woodland Beach. Then again, some of them may be planning to board the hayride trains of flatcars that also ran to the shore at that time. Or perhaps they're still searching for some of the pirate treasure said to have been buried there so many years before. Long before Woodland Beach became a popular seaside resort, legend has it that Captain Kidd favored the site as a good place to bury treasure.

Wandering Witches

Did a family of witches once reside in Newark? And were they murdered by members of their own family? Residents report that six pale figures can sometimes be seen walking along Salem Church Road at night. The story goes that the entire family was hanged for practicing witchcraft in the early 1900s and are still seeking revenge on the relatives responsible for their demise.

Mad Dog

The legend of a demon dog has long been a part of European folklore. Originally taken from Norse mythology, in which the dog was the black hound of the god Odin, the story was brought by early Viking invaders to England, where, for centuries, the demon dog has haunted lonely country roads and isolated graveyards. The tale eventually emigrated to America and lives on even today.

Local residents warn that it pays to drive carefully when you're on State Route 12, west of Frederica, especially on rainy nights. That's where the old Bonwell House still stands at Andrews Lake. Legend has it that the spirit of a huge wild dog with glowing red eyes and a bushy tail, known locally as the Fence Rail Dog, can be seen on stormy nights running along the road. The creature, so christened because it was reportedly as long as a fence rail, is said by some to be the ghost of a young slave who was killed about two hundred years ago by his abusive owner, Michael Bonwell. Apparently, Bonwell remorselessly disposed of the young man's body by grinding it with his corn crop in the gristmill that he owned. Although everyone in the neighborhood knew that he had committed murder, Bonwell escaped being tried for the crime because authorities could not locate the youth's body.

Afterward, the other slaves reportedly said that they could sense the youth's presence from time to time, as though he were seeking a final resting place. Bonwell, however, apparently remained untroubled by his heinous crime until his death. His constant cruelty, which continued even after he killed the young slave, was so well known that it is said that his neighbors refused to attend his funeral when he died. But his slaves buried his body properly, although in an unmarked grave, perhaps hoping to appease the spirit of Bonwell's victim. Despite their efforts, the red-eyed dog continued to haunt the region around Bonwell House, perhaps hoping to find the location of his murderer's grave.

In another version of the story, the dog's spirit won't rest because his owner was murdered by an angry tenant, who then ground up the landlord's body with cornmeal and fed it to the dog. Still another says that the dog is the ghost of the tenant, who was transformed after he died because of his heinous deed.

Little Boy Ghost

Locust Grove Farm in Middletown is more than 150 years old, but its resident ghost is a child. The house is believed to be haunted by the spirit of a boy who died there in the early twentieth century. Over the years, occupants of the farm have reported sensing a presence lingering there and hearing noises in the night. Like many young ghosts who died during that period, the boy apparently is fascinated by modern technology. Both televisions and lights have been repeatedly turned on and off, and toys suddenly move for no apparent reason.

The Lonely Lighthouse Keeper

During the late eighteenth and early nineteenth centuries, Delaware authorities constructed twenty-seven lighthouses to help guide commercial and passenger vessels through the not always placid waters along the coast of the Delaware River and Bay. Nine remain standing. Several of the lighthouses have been converted by private owners into museums, but most are still in active use. The structures ranged dramatically in design, from the tall, round brick tower that rises over Fenwick Island to the homier lighthouses that were not markedly different from other houses in a seaside town. Some were situated offshore, with the only means of access by water when the tides rose.

For generations, the lights were operated by lighthouse keepers, men who sometimes endured weeks of loneliness at their often isolated posts. One such solitary spot was the Fourteen Foot Bank Lighthouse, located several miles off Bowers Beach in the Delaware Bay. The first lighthouse in America to be built on a submarine base, its light first shone out across the dangerous shoals on December 1, 1886. Although topped with a cast-iron Victorian-style "house" that included a "backyard" privy, one lighthouse keeper apparently found the post too much to bear.

In *Lighthouses of New Jersey & Delaware: History, Mystery, Legends & Lore,* author Bob Trapani Jr. notes that Lewes native Lewis Robinson was employed in 1910 as an assistant lighthouse keeper at Fourteen Foot Bank. That winter, Robinson suffered a serious fall that miraculously resulted in just bruises and a broken ankle. But he endured terrible pain for several weeks because he was unable to receive immediate medical attention. During that time of year, few boats traveled past the lighthouse. Those that did either did not see or chose to ignore the keeper's efforts to draw help. When a boat finally arrived and took him to shore, Robinson's ankle was set, but other, more serious damage had already been done.

Although he eventually resumed his duties as keeper, apparently just being aboard the isolated lighthouse was more than Robinson could stand. The trauma of the fall apparently haunted him until he finally succumbed. In June 1911, his fellow keepers were shocked to hear him screaming from the top of the structure. They arrived to discover that he had swallowed carbolic acid and watched him die a slow, wrenching death. Robinson's body was removed to land by one of the other keepers. But some area residents say that there are warm summer nights when vessels traveling past the Fourteen Foot Bank Lighthouse can still hear his horrifying cries.

The War Wraiths

Located at the end of State Route 36, about seven miles east of Milford, is the ominous-sounding Slaughter Beach, home of Fort Salisbury. Although originally meant to serve as a coastal defense against a German invasion during World War I, the fort was not constructed until 1917. Stripped of its armory, it remained empty and unused until the advent of World War II, when it was used to house Italian and German prisoners of war. A few years after the war ended, the fort was abandoned once again, and today it is privately owned by a local farmer.

Visitors who have been permitted inside the menacing concrete bunker say, however, that the presence of the former prisoners is still felt there in the old cell blocks that line the front bunker. The fort is also marked by cold spots, a familiar sign of restless supernatural energy.

Murder in Omar

Nothing remains of the tiny hamlet of Omar, which once stood on Clarksville Road west of Frankford. Nothing, that is, except the spirit of a murder victim whose sole crime was attempting to look out for the welfare of another family member. The year was 1927, a roaring time of bootlegging, robbery, and other criminal activity just before the official arrival of the Great Depression. Living conditions were hard for everyone in the small town, and Mary Carey wanted more than Omar had to offer. She decided that the quickest route to improving her life would be to murder her brother, Robert Hitchens. Mary knew that she stood to inherit a substantial sum of money as the sole beneficiary named on his life insurance policy.

It was in early November that Mary persuaded her two older sons, Howard and James, to help her commit the heinous crime. If successful, she promised, they would receive a new car. The trio apparently arrived one night at Hitchens's house, where they beat and finally shot him to death. When Hitchens failed to report for work a few days later, a neighbor discovered his dead body stretched out on the living room rug. The presence of a whiskey bottle close by the body caused police to conclude that Hitchens had been the victim of a gang of bootleggers.

Seven years later, however, Mary's youngest son attempted to gain leniency from the police for his own petty crimes by confessing that he had overheard his mother and brothers discussing Hitchens's murder. The three culprits were soon arrested and tried for their crime. Although the jury recommended mercy, Mary and Howard were hanged, and James was given a life sentence. For many years after the criminals were brought to justice, local residents claimed they could sense a presence hovering around the victim's house. Perhaps it was impossible for Robert Hitchens's spirit to rest, knowing that his murderers had been members of his own family.

Spirits of the Swamp

The Cypress Swamp Conservation Area lies near Gumboro, on the borders of Delaware and Maryland. It is also known locally as the Great Pocomoke Swamp, Big Cypress, or Burnt Swamp because of a fire that smoldered there for about a year in the 1930s. No one knows for sure how it started, but some area residents speculate that the fire was generated by an explosion at one of the many illegal stills that operated there during Prohibition. When the first still burned, it set off the others, and the fire spread rapidly through the rest of the swamp. It had been a dry year, and the flames traveled underground through the tangle of roots and vegetation, destroying peat beds, stands of trees, and nearby cornfields.

Although the present-day conservation area is just a fraction of the swamp's original size, it still shelters a wide variety of flora and fauna, including cypress, cedar, and gum trees and turtles, snakes, and frogs. Once a well-known source of cypress timber, the swamp is reputed to now offer a different kind of crop. A number of spirits have been reported throughout the area over the years, ranging from the benign ghost of an elderly shingle maker, still determined to sell his products, to the horrifying Swamp Creature—perhaps, like the Cape Henlopen Devil, yet another descendant of the Jersey Devil. The shingle maker is said to still ply his trade on dark, cloudy days, because he believes that machine-produced shingles are inferior to his hand-turned ones.

There was some speculation during the 1920s that the Swamp Creature may just have been a costumed prankster on the loose, scaring local residents who passed through the region. But after a number of half-eaten dog carcasses were discovered on the edge of the swamp, area residents decided that some kind of creature definitely had to be lingering within the marshes. Some speculated that it may have been a bear, but others said it was a wild-eyed, hairy monster hiding in the trees. And some say he is living there still.

The Springer Heirs

Wills have long been disputed by disgruntled heirs, certain they should have received more from the estate of the deceased. Few such documents, however, were contested as long as that of Charles

Christopher Springer, whose division of property was questioned for more than two hundred years.

It seems that after Springer died, a group of unscrupulous promoters convinced family members that he had been not just wealthy, but also a member of Swedish aristocracy. His estate reportedly was valued between $80 million and $150 million. The heirs were gathered, and in a show of good faith, they paid a small fortune to the promoters to help establish their claim through the courts. But the promoters disappeared with their money, and legal documentation proved that Springer's land was in reality the property of Old Swedes Church. One swindler finally confessed to his part in the elaborate plot to bilk the family members of their money, but Springer descendants continued to try to press their claim well into the 1930s.

Invitations to a Funeral

The small port settlement on Little Duck Creek (known today as the Smyrna River) was christened Fast Landing when it was founded in 1723. Close to a hundred years later, it was thriving enough to be renamed Leipsic in honor of the town of Leipzig, a center of fur shipping in Germany. During the nineteenth century, the Delaware community maintained a boat-building industry and marketed oysters, salt hay, tomatoes, and peaches. Leipsic also thrived as a hunting ground for muskrat, a local delicacy that was shipped to restaurants throughout the state.

Today the population numbers only a little more than two hundred residents living in fewer than a hundred houses. But Leipsic is still the place where trappers head between December and March to catch muskrats, which remain a popular dish for regional residents. Other customs were also retained in the small community long after they had disappeared elsewhere, such as the practice of having a family member of a deceased person going from door to door with pieces of paper bearing the place and time of the funeral. Everyone received one, even strangers who may not have known the individual who died.

Folk Superstitions

As in most American states, folk customs brought from Europe spread rapidly through Delaware. Many of these superstitions continued to be practiced in the countryside long after they had been dismissed by residents of cities and towns. *Delaware: A Guide to the First State* reports that in 1938, many rural residents still believed that if a knife, fork, or spoon was dropped, it meant that a visitor was coming—a man, woman, or child, respectively. After a wedding was held in some parts of the state the first things carried over the threshold of the couple's new house were the family Bible and a salt shaker.

It was thought advisable to wear or carry chalcedony or obsidian to keep ghosts away. Silver was also considered to be an effective deterrent against restless spirits, and iron, from a simple household item like a pair of scissors to a piece of farm equipment, was supposed to keep malevolent spirits from causing harm. Perhaps one reason that cast iron became popular in so many households was because it served this purpose as well. In *The Encyclopedia of Ghosts and Spirits*, Rosemary Ellen Guiley notes: "An iron rod placed on a grave will prevent a ghost from rising out of the ground, and an iron horseshoe hung over a doorway will prevent a ghost from entering a house, stable or building."

Other beliefs were adopted from Native American traditions. Some country dwellers maintained that the mournful cry of the whippoorwill was really that of a restless spirit, bemoaning the fact that it had left too many things undone before it died. Guiley states that some thought "whippoorwills are not birds at all, but disembodied spirits that can never be caught, the proof being that the sound retreats as a person approaches it."

The Mysterious Lotus Lily Beds

A familiar midwestern legend credits "Johnny Appleseed" with planting apple trees throughout the territory. But the lotus lily beds that once grew profusely in Jones Creek just north of Lebanon reportedly had a much more exotic origin. Some local residents once believed that the lilies' seeds had been brought from Canada, but others preferred to credit Egypt as the source of their origin.

The second version caught local imagination after the sunken hull of a ship covered with Egyptian hieroglyphs and symbols was supposedly discovered in the creek. The lilies, said to have floated from the hull, took root in the water's rich soil, where they flourished through the late 1930s. Unfortunately, no one was ever able to locate the remains of the ship to verify whether some long-dead Egyptian explorer actually sailed to the coast of the New World. But the lilies, for generations, were an exotic reminder of a mystery that remained unsolved.

The Seven Whistlers and the Merman

Sailing was an extremely hazardous occupation well into the nineteenth century, with ships at the mercy of sometimes treacherous waters when they left port. As a result, sailors developed their own superstitions designed to ward off evil and keep luck close until they returned safely home from their months-long journeys. After all, it was difficult to say when an evil harbinger such as the Seven Whistlers might appear. These ghostly birds, sometimes believed to be the spirits of drowned seamen, usually flew by at night with shrill, eerie cries. They were believed to herald forthcoming death or disaster. Another ill omen was the arrival of an albatross, also said to be the carrier of a drowned sailor's soul, whose appearance foretold the arrival of a coming storm.

So to ward off disaster, the sailors tattooed their skin with protective images, wore golden earrings, and whenever possible, kept an amulet handily within reach in a pocket. One such lucky talisman, which first appeared in America around 1822, was a tiny, dried object that appeared to be part human and part fish, said to be a merman. These mermen apparently were purchased from Japanese seamen, who carried them for good luck.

By 1844, the colorful showman P. T. Barnum (1810–91) had bought a merman for his New York exhibit of curiosities, labeling it the "Feejee Mermaid." Its popularity spread throughout the country when his carnival toured the United States. By the twentieth century, however, the merman—like most of Barnum's exhibits—had become little more than a dim memory for the general public. That is, unless you live in or travel to Lewes. It seems that the Zwaanendael Museum has had a merman on display since 1941, when it was originally loaned by the family of a local sea captain. The foot-long creature, considered an integral part of the maritime history of Sussex County, became a part of the permanent collection in 1985, when it was purchased by the museum for $250.

Wartime Memories

The Dover Air Force Base has been an important military facility since it opened in 1941. There, generations of pilots, technicians, and other personnel trained and maintained the craft that were used during combat. On the base, in a restored World War II Army Air Force Rocket Test Center, is the Air Mobility Command Museum, where one can find the history of the base, along with archival military records from throughout the United States. The museum, open to the public, also houses a growing collection of planes, including a B-17 Flying Fortress, a P-51 Mustang, and the first C-141A Starfire ever built. It also seems to be occasionally visited by a ghost.

Michael Leister, director of the museum, considers himself to be a skeptic when the subject turns to the supernatural. Though he concedes that at night the aged, dimly lit hangar that houses the museum does creak and groan, and the mannequins used for exhibits sometimes appear to move, he attributes anything that might seem unusual to others to more earthly sources. Nevertheless, some people beleive that the AMC Museum is in fact home to the ghost of former Technical Sgt. Winfrid "Bing" Wood, who appears from time to time because he has fond memories of the airplane in which he served during World War II. According to Leister, Wood loved the C-47 Turf and Sport Special that is now housed at the museum. During his lifetime, Wood, the aerial engineer assigned to the plane, visited the museum on several occasions to watch his plane being restored. A true character, he would share stories with Leister and the staff about his wartime experiences, such as the day after D-Day, when he was almost struck by some shrapnel that passed through the fuselage while they were flying over St. Mère Église in France, dropping supplies to waiting American troops. When the mission ended, it was Wood's job to repair the damage to the plane.

According to several people who have worked at the museum, Wood's attachment to the C-47 continued into the afterlife. Two former Air Force historians employed at the museum claimed that they saw Wood on several occasions after his death in 1992. To confirm their sightings, the museum allowed some paranormal researchers to spend the night inside the museum. They claimed to have registered high levels of spectral activity, but Leister, ever the skeptic, remains unconvinced. "In all this time since his passing, he has never come to visit me," he says, "but I wish he could. I would be happy to have the opportunity to sit and listen to an old friend relate more of his adventures during World War II."

The Ghosts of Abbott's Mill

Multiple hauntings have been reported to occur at places that have seen a lot of life. Some seem to be gentle spirits that simply are reluctant to leave a familiar place where they have been happy; in other cases, the ghosts prefer to torment those whom they perceive as trespassing on their various domains. One such location is Abbott's Mill near Milford, a historic site that today is used as a nature center by the Delaware Nature Society.

The three-story mill building, which stands in a picturesque meadow by a pond, is believed to date from the late eighteenth century. In the early 1800s, it belonged to William Johnson, a lawyer from Dover, who apparently was not interested in operating the mill for profit. Some local residents have said that he spent a lot of time in a small, blue bedroom on the second floor of the house situated there and that his ghost still resides in the room today. Former owners reported that anyone who attempted to sleep in the room would get the uncomfortable sensation of the hair standing up on the back of his neck. During a séance they conducted to contact Johnson, they learned that he, in fact, was not planning to leave anytime soon. He was so happy there in his lifetime that he saw no reason to depart the premises just because he died.

Over the years, other ghostly presences have manifested themselves. Lights, where no lights should be shining, have appeared in both the mill and the house. Abbott's Mill is said to have been a stop on the Underground Railroad, one that unfortunately was well known to the raiders who chased down runaway slaves, and one spirit seems to be that of a hapless slave who reportedly was killed there while trying to escape north. His ghost is said to linger in a small compartment hidden under one of the third-floor storage bins.

A Confederate soldier is also believed to hover at Abbott's Mill, but little is known about why his presence manifests itself there. One night, a young guest approached the owner and said that someone was locked inside the mill and pounding on the door to get out. When the owner questioned the child, he accurately described the soldier, who had been seen by others on previous occasions. In addition, the property is apparently haunted by the spirit of a youth who was said to have drowned in the pond. During a séance, the boy indicated that he was planning to leave the mill eventually, but for now he was happy to linger there.

A Milford resident who had never placed much stock in the supernatural had occasion to recant his words on the night of October 27, 1945. The man recalled that he was driving toward Abbott's Mill Pond late that night when he saw a lone figure standing by the side of the road. When he realized that it was a young woman, he stopped and chivalrously offered her a ride home. The woman, dripping wet and looking sad, climbed into the car but refused to divulge anything more than her address.

To keep her warm, the man placed his coat over her shoulders and headed toward the heart of Milford, where the woman said she lived. Upon their arrival, she thanked him for his assistance and ran into the house. Curious about the strange incident, it wasn't until he had driven some distance that the man realized he had left his coat behind. Early the following morning, he drove back to the house and knocked on the door. When it was opened, the man explained why he was there, but the occupant's response was completely unexpected.

The old man who lived at the house angrily accused him of playing a cruel joke. His daughter, he declared, was not driven home the preceding night. It was, in fact, the first anniversary of his daughter's death. Despondent over her lover, the young woman had committed suicide—by drowning herself in Abbott's Mill Pond.

Shocked by the older man's words, the man returned home but received another surprise two days later. That was when the young woman's father appeared on his doorstep, holding the missing overcoat. It seems that he had found it draped across the headstone of his daughter's grave.

The Cossart Road Cult House

Are some places inherently evil? Can a house learn bad behavior from its occupants or even draw evil from the ground on which it is built? Anyone who has seen the film *The Amityville Horror* or *Poltergeist* knows that some believe it's possible. And those who have visited the Cossart Road Cult House don't doubt that it's true.

The Cult House, also known regionally as the Hell House or the Devil House, lies tucked in a corner of the Brandywine River Valley where a vast amount of malevolent energy supposedly lurks. In the 1950s, the house was reportedly the place where local Ku Klux Klan members met to plan their raids and hang their human "trophies" on spikes that lined a wooden fence. Before long, the road leading to the house was said to be haunted by the spirits of those who had been murdered. Anyone who made the mistake of traveling there after dark could hear the cries and screams of the departed, along with the creaks of the ropes to which they were bound. The house later was thought to be used by Satanists as a place of ritual sacrifice.

Some say that evil has existed there for centuries. Others feel that it emanated from the road that ran through that portion of the valley. It apparently was so strong that even the trees were stunted by it. But regardless of the source of whatever wrongs have occurred there over the years, locals say that the Cult House is not a place you want to stay in—or even around—for very long, whether it's day or night.

Fairy Sightings

Although fairies have developed a reputation in recent years as being benevolent, gentle woodland spirits, they were known for centuries as malicious sprites given to creating all kinds of mischief. Vain and self-centered, they were believed by some cultures to resent humans because their own civilization of tiny beings no longer walked the earth. Others though they were not humanoid at all, but either the spirits of those who had died too soon or perhaps fallen angels. Whatever their origin, the "little people," as they were also known, had the power to cause great misfortune to anyone who failed to treat them with proper respect. Fairy rings, circles of dark grass where they allegedly met under a full moon, were considered especially dangerous places to cross, especially after dark.

Like many familiar European folktales, stories of fairies crossed the Atlantic in the eighteenth and nineteenth centuries. It made sense then to leave a bit of food on the doorstep or by the fireplace hearth if it ensured the goodwill of the tiny folk. Some people find these legends intriguing even today. One young Wilmington woman recently reported at www.fairygardens.com that her longstanding interest in fairies was rewarded about two years ago. It was late at night, she was the only person awake in the house, and she heard the sound of children laughing in the otherwise empty room where she had been watching television. Frightened at first, she eventually became certain that her cheerful nocturnal visitors were in fact fairies. Although she did not make contact with them then, she remains hopeful that they will return one day.

Red Hannah

Like most American states, Delaware was settled by people who believed that any crime, no matter how small, frequently merited severe punishment. But long after most other states had turned away from harsh methods of punishment, Delaware seemed content to maintain stringent measures, such as the six combination stocks and whipping posts erected throughout the state. The most notorious of them, dubbed Red Hannah by African American prisoners who were ordered to "embrace" the post, was originally erected at the Kent County Jail in Dover in the eighteenth century.

Although whipping was condemned as barbaric and outlawed in Pennsylvania as early as 1794, the last public whipping occurred in Delaware in 1952, even though many residents of the First State condemned such punishment. In fact, whipping remained on state statutes for another twenty years. Together with neighboring Maryland, Delaware was one of the last two states to allow this form of corporal punishment. Dr. Robert G. Caldwell, a sociology professor at the University of Delaware, was so outraged by the practice that he wrote a book titled Red Hannah in 1947, condemning the practice of public whipping.

On rare occasions, the prisoners themselves actively fought back against the use of the whip. One New Castle man who was to receive five lashes for his crimes struggled so much in his shackles that the sheriff missed the last stroke. The officer then gave him a sixth blow that the prisoner later protested all the way to the Delaware Supreme Court. Although the judges considered the man's claim to be valid, they ruled that since he would probably wind up back in prison before long, he was entitled to claim credit for already having received one lash.

Red Hannah and her siblings were removed from public view many years ago, but some residents of larger cities and towns say that their legacy lingers on. There are nights when the whistling sound of the lash and an accompanying cry can sometimes be heard in public squares where they once stood. Perhaps the victims' ghosts are in too much pain to find any lasting rest.

The Silk King

Almost forty years have passed since James H. W. Thompson disappeared into the vast jungles of Malaysia. A variety of books and documentaries about the mysterious fate of this charismatic figure continue to be produced even today, each with its own theory. But it is unlikely that anyone will ever know what really happened to the Delaware native, who would come to be internationally known as Thailand's "Silk King."

Thompson was born in 1906 into an upper-income family in the affluent community of Greenville, located northwest of Wilmington. A 1928 graduate of Princeton University, he later studied architecture at the University of Pennsylvania. Although he was firmly established in a successful career, Thompson decided to join the Office of Strategic Services (OSS), the forerunner of the Central Intelligence Agency (CIA), at the advent of World War II. He parachuted into the northern reaches of Thailand in 1945 to help raise resistance against the Japanese. Thompson's mission abruptly ended when the Japanese surrendered, but he found himself drawn to the warm, exotic country. When he received his discharge the following year, he quickly returned to Thailand and began traveling through it to learn more about its people and their culture.

While exploring Bangkok, Thompson noticed that its once-thriving silk industry had all but disappeared. In a poor district known as Ban Krua, however, he found a whole community of weavers who pursued their craft as a sideline, weaving raw textured silk into traditional designs. Thompson began to visit them on a regular basis and persuaded them to start producing silk for his new venture, Thai Silk Company Ltd. Although the residents of Ban Krua were at first skeptical of the tall westerner's ideas, their work was well received when Thompson brought samples to America. Before long, the demand for Thai silk was so great that other manufacturers were encouraged to produce it as well.

Then, while on vacation in Malaysia's remote Camaron Highlands in March 1967, Thompson suddenly disappeared. Although local authorities searched the surrounding wilderness for months afterward, no one could find any evidence of what had happened to Thailand's "Silk King." Speculation about his true fate continues even today. Was he kidnapped by Communists? Was he killed by bandits or business rivals? Did he simply walk off into the jungle to enjoy a simpler life among the natives? The mystery remains unsolved nearly four decades later.

The Phantom Housekeeper

Delaware author Bill Frank has documented many reported ghostly occurrences in the First State. One such story that was related to him focused on a restless spirit who wanted nothing more than to help one harried mother with her housework. The woman and her family had moved in the spring of 1973 to a farmhouse just a few miles south of Camden. An older home, it required weeks of cleaning and maintenance in order to make it habitable for its new owners. But the family soon discovered, once the painting and plastering were out of the way, that they loved the peace and quiet of their new residence.

The front room was especially cozy, thanks to a large fireplace that occupied one wall, but the woman realized that the strenuous job of cleaning the hearth was not one she was going to enjoy. She kept postponing the task until, one night, she promised herself that it would be the first thing she tackled the next morning. According to Frank: "She arose before seven and went about the morning chores, then turned to the fireplace. To her surprise, it was spotless, brass shining like a mirror, hearth swept bare, looking as though someone had spent hours on it."

But how could this be? The children were all in bed. Perhaps her husband had pitched in as a surprise before he left for work. When questioned that night, however, he denied all knowledge of the incident. The family began teasing the mother about her invisible housekeeper, but she learned not to take the subject lightly a few weeks later. When the fireplace hearth became dirty again, the woman demanded that the ghost get to work. She arose the next morning to find soot and ashes scattered all over the rugs and furniture. After that, the woman refrained from any type of comment. And the fireplace hearth reportedly was cleaned by ghostly hands on a regular basis.

The Ghostly Host

Do some people just attract ghosts? Is psychic energy genetic? Some say that there are people who are "ghost magnets," with the extrasensory perception to see beyond existing dimensions. One such person may have been Hilda Chance, who reportedly saw spirits in just about every home she ever owned.

According to Adi-Kent Thomas Jeffrey in *Ghosts in the Valley*, Hilda's ability may have been handed down from her mother. Jeffrey relates:

> One of the eeriest incidents happened in her girlhood home in Harrington, Delaware. Hilda's mother awoke early one morning as her husband lay peacefully sleeping beside her, when she heard the catch of the bedroom door click open and someone walk in.
>
> She could hardly believe what she saw. It was the figure of her husband coming into the room. He was carrying a suitcase.
>
> Quickly she glanced over at the form beside her. Her husband was obviously there and deep asleep.

When Hilda's mother later questioned her husband, he denied that he was planning to take a trip. But before long, he was in fact required to go out of town. Just as her vision foretold, she saw him return with his suitcase. And shortly thereafter, he died.

Hilda, who moved to Pennsylvania after she married, was visited by the spirits of former residents of the different houses wherever she moved. Her supernatural roommates included children and women, who occasionally rearranged the furniture if they didn't approve of the changes made by the Chances. According to Jeffrey,

Hilda simply accepted the appearance of the ghosts without question. Like a gracious host, she made them feel comfortable in their surroundings even after death.

UFO Sightings

The Air Force Base at Dover has recorded a number of UFO sightings by both qualified pilots, trained to expect the unexpected, and civilians, who have been startled by brilliant spheres rapidly crisscrossing the night skies. In some instances, the presence of the craft is easily explained; in others, it poses more of a mystery. One puzzling sighting occurred in Delaware long before sky traffic was commonplace. A few years ago, a young man who was in the process of restoring an old farmhouse near the Dover Air Force Base reported that he had discovered a farmer's diary entry dating from Saturday, February 11, 1905, citing the appearance of a UFO. The night was described in the almanac portion of the journal as cold, clear, and moonlit, and the entry for that date states concisely: "I saw an equal sided triangle object drift away from the moon and disappear in a few, perhaps 10 seconds, it looked like a banner." No further information on this sighting was recorded, but many other unidentified flying objects have been reported by the residents of the First State.

Project Blue Book, the Air Force's official UFO study program between 1952 and 1969, documented that on July 27, 1952, at approximately 5 P.M, a UFO was spotted over Wilmington. Twelve years later, two Air Force pilots flying east of Dover reported that a blurry round object was on a direct collision course with their transport plane. The pilots, who maintained visual contact with the object for about two minutes, were able to evade it and watched, amazed, as it sped off into the distance.

For many years after that, UFO sightings were not always documented by government agencies or individuals. But in 1985, on a cold November night, a Delaware state police dispatcher received reports that a UFO was hovering over Georgetown. When a police helicopter was sent out to investigate, the officers stated that they could find no evidence of a saucer. The director of emergency services for Sussex County later revealed that he had received three telephone calls from folks who claimed to have sighted a ball of light with orange streamers on it.

In 1998, radio talk-show host Dan Gaffney of station WGMD in Rehoboth Beach received more than fifty calls from nervous residents who reported seeing UFOs in Sussex County. The callers described bright lights, sometimes blue or white or green, flashing from round objects between the towns of Milford and Bethany Beach.

The Corpse Light

Delaware has a number of lighthouses still in operation along its eastern seaboard, protecting ships that may wander off course near its treacherous coastline. Thus a light sometimes seen flashing from Cape Henlopen State Park might not seem unusual, except for one detail: No lighthouse was ever built on this section of the coast—at least, not by human hands. Cape Henlopen is said to be home to the "corpse light," a phantom lighthouse that appears in the night to lure unsuspecting sailors to their doom. The corpse light allegedly was conjured by a local tribe after British soldiers invaded a marriage ceremony and massacred many of the Indians present. Their curse called for a drum of stone that would signal death to the Europeans and destruction to the ships that brought them to American shores.

The corpse light, first sighted more than 250 years ago, is held responsible for the sinking of the *Devonshireman* on December 25, 1655. The ship followed a beacon of light from a cylindrical shaft of stone that the crew mistakenly thought was a lighthouse and plowed into the rocks, killing about two hundred people on board. Another victim of the corpse light was the British sloop *deBraak*, which was lured to its doom on May 25, 1778. Area residents say that on moonless nights, the phantom ship sometimes reappears and reenacts the disaster. The ghost of its captain, James Drew, has also been seen leaving the cemetery at St. Peters Church in Lewes, where his body is buried, to search for his long-lost crew.

In 1800, many witnesses reported that they had seen an Indian perched on a column of stone just before a passenger barge rammed into the rocks, killing many of those on board. Even modern technology apparently could not prevent the corpse light from claiming its victims. The USS *Poet*, a twelve thousand-ton grain carrier, reportedly vanished without a trace off the coast in 1980. Authorities believe that the ship, actually being used to transport heroin, was diverted by hijackers to the Middle East; however, no sighting of it has been documented for more than twenty years.

Cape Henlopen is located at the end of State Route 404, seventeen miles northeast of Georgetown.

The Sea Witch

More than two hundred years have passed since HMS *deBraak* foundered in the waters off Cape Henlopen, the victim of a violent storm. Since then, the cape's stillness has been occasionally shattered by the piercing screams of a phantom called the Sea Witch or the Bad Weather Witch by the locals. She apparently has appointed herself the guardian of the sunken ship, which was said to be carrying millions in treasure, and patrols the coast at night. Although several centuries have passed, the witch still feels compelled to maintain her vigil.

Some fishermen unwillingly made her acquaintance one night while walking along the beach. They reported that the quiet night was broken by the sound of a woman screaming a little farther along the shore. As they watched, an ancient, wild-eyed apparition with bedraggled hair ran toward them, screaming "Don't go near the water! Keep away!" Dumbstruck, the men were unable to move. She ran past them shrieking, but as the men turned, they discovered that they were alone once more on the beach. The woman had vanished.

The *deBraak*, which sank off the Delaware coast on May 25, 1798, has always puzzled historians and treasure hunters who have sought to learn more about the ship. Some believe that the crew consisted of British pirates, who successfully plied their trade throughout the Caribbean. The weight of millions of dollars' worth of jewels, gold, and silver in the hold was believed to be responsible for causing the ship to sink, less than a mile from shore, during the storm. Over the years, efforts were made periodically to raise the ship from the depths but were unsuccessful—perhaps hampered by the witch's presence? In *Ghost Stories of the Delaware Coast,* authors David J. Seibold and Charles J. Adams III recount: "In 1935, an expedition led by Charles Colstad and Richard Wilson was one of the best-financed failures in the search for the *deBraak* treasure. So frustrated by the failure were some of the salvagers that they actually fabricated an effigy of the Bad Weather Witch, blasted it with rounds of gunfire, burned it and tossed it overboard."

It wasn't until 1986 that modern technology allowed divers to recover parts of the ship and some of the wealth that had lain beneath the waves for so long. In addition to the remains of the *deBraak*, they salvaged a historic treasure trove of coins, buttons, jewelry, and other objects, which have since been placed on exhibit at the Zwaanendael Museum. Although some researchers believe that everything worth saving has been brought up from the waters of the bay, others occasionally toy with the idea that there is still more treasure to be found. However, their enthusiasm undoubtedly is dampened by the thought of an encounter with the witch, who is said to maintain her solitary vigil along the shore.

The Ghost of Wish Sheppard

The Caroline County Jail in Denton, Maryland, lies just fifteen miles west of Harrington. Also classified as a federal facility, it has on more than one occasion housed inmates from Delaware, who are usually serving time on income tax evasion charges. And some of them soon discovered that they were serving time with a ghost.

The Caroline County Jail reportedly was haunted by the spirit of Wish Sheppard, an eighteen-year-old who was executed for sexually assaulting a fifteen-year-old girl. The year was 1915. Although Sheppard maintained his innocence to the end, he was still hanged for the crime. For many years afterward, his ghost apparently chose to torment both his fellow prisoners and the sheriff's officers who guarded the jail. In earlier times, inmates reported that the ghost would grab at their clothing or throw their personal belongings from the cell windows. On more recent occasions, the guards claimed to see Sheppard's silent shadow moving throughout uninhabited rooms. Then, they said, the jail's elevator would suddenly start, even when no human hand was present to push the buttons; freshly painted rooms would be smeared by unseen hands; and the closed-circuit television monitors would malfunction for no apparent reason.

Sheriff Louis C. Andrew claimed that what seemed to be a handprint kept appearing in the hallway near the room where Sheppard was executed. Although painted over many times, it always re-emerged. Sheppard's spirit seemed to go dormant when the jail was remodeled in the early 1980s. Perhaps he managed to find a previously inaccessible escape route and has made his way to a more welcoming home.

Some Haunted Houses and Other Scary Places

Though not every supernatural sighting in Delaware has been recorded, a number of homes and hotels have been reported to have their share of paranormal activity.

The Cannonball House, on Front Street in Lewes, was built in 1743 and currently serves as a nautical museum. It received its name after a cannonball from a British frigate lodged in the wall in 1813. Although no one knows why, the ghost who resides there apparently refuses to let the door to the second-floor loft stay closed.

The Addy-Sea Inn in Bethany Beach was built as a family residence in 1904 by John Addy, a plumber from Pittsburgh who wanted to settle in what was then an isolated area. He was forced to move the house twice in the 1920s, however, after it was battered by severe coastal storms. Today the inn is an elegant Victorian bed-and-breakfast replete with antique furnishings, tin ceilings, and nineteenth-century artwork. It's a wonderful place to unwind, as long as you don't occupy Room 1, 6, or 11, which are reportedly haunted by different spirits—including a deceased former employee. Witnesses have told of strange occurrences, including a vibrating bathtub and eerie organ music in Rooms 1 and 6. A former handyman named Paul Delaney, who once made a name for himself as a swimmer, is said to make his presence known to visitors in Room 11. He has been seen standing next to or sitting on the bed there.

Pachette Playhouse in Delaware City was last used as a dance hall in 1999, but the supernatural activity that occurred there was so obvious it eventually frightened away the partiers. Among the strange occurrences were bleeding mirrors, figures in paintings and photographs coming to life, and a malevolent invisible force pushing unsuspecting clubgoers down the front steps. A strange violet light has also been reported in the upstairs rooms, highlighting faces that perhaps danced there a century or two ago.

Visitors to the **Blue Coat Inn** in Dover have told of nighttime patrols conducted by the ghosts of Col. John Haslett and a young drummer boy, who stand guard against a British invasion.

Another well-known haunted house in Dover is the **Dickinson Mansion,** where the son of the original owner seems reluctant to move on even today. Local attorney John Dickinson apparently prefers to linger in the old brick plantation house built in 1740 by his father, Judge Samuel Dickinson. John and his brother Philemon were well-respected members of the community. But while Philemon is resting in peace, it seems that John, known as the "penman of the Revolutionary War" because of his patriotic writings, still roams the halls of his boyhood home. Bed linens are frequently found in disarray, because John apparently still enjoys an afternoon nap as he did when he was alive. Besides the master bedroom, he is believed to haunt the book room near the entrance hall. Paranormal researchers, armed with tape recorders, have heard the scratchy sound of a quill pen writing on parchment coming from that area, as though Dickinson remains determined to get his thoughts down. Is he reliving happy or unhappy memories? It is likely that no one will ever know. The Dickinson Mansion, located seven miles southeast of Dover near Kitts Hummock Road, is currently operated by the Delaware State Museums.

A privately owned, early-nineteenth-century home in New Castle's **Battery Park** is said to be haunted by the ghost of a woman who does not always seem too pleased with the way "her" home is being kept. The dishes have been rearranged in the kitchen cupboards, without visible assistance, and occasionally fly off the shelves if they are not kept in what she feels is proper fashion. Other household items have been moved on tables and shelves and are repeatedly returned to their original positions if someone else moves them. Such incidents occurred often enough to send one cleaning woman out the door.

Despite the minor disagreements over the way the house is kept, the current resident believed he received a supernatural seal of approval one day from the resident spirit when he found a sterling silver wedding band on the floor of the bathroom. Not long afterward, the owner saw the figure of a woman standing in the yard, watching him garden. She appeared to be about thirty and was dressed in Colonial-style clothing. He glanced away for just a moment, and when he looked back, the woman was gone.

The mansion that sits on **McColley Pond** outside Frederica is believed to be haunted by the ghost of a young slave, who reportedly jumped to her death from an attic window after she had been confined to the upper levels of the house as punishment for resisting the advances of her owner. Some local residents say that on moonless nights, the sound of a woman screaming can be heard echoing in the vicinity of the house.

In Woonsocket, the fourth floor of the **Mount Saint Charles Academy** is said to be haunted by a former brother of the Order of the Sacred Heart, who once ran the high school. Legend has it that the students were so afraid of this man that they retaliated only after he died, sticking pencils into his eyes during his viewing. But their actions apparently outraged the brother even further. Since then, the students—and those who came after—found themselves confronted by his angry ghost, who walks at will in and out of their rooms.

The property known simply as the **Old Homestead,** at the heart of Gumboro, is believed to harbor some spirits who can be heard breathing on the staircase or walking through the yard. But their presence is welcome by the local population, because residents believe the ghosts have helped protect the Homestead from developers.

Lewes is home to a number of contemporary developments, including the **Neighborhood of Bay Oaks,** where evidence has been found of a battle between the local Indians and Dutch settlers. Locals have seen streaks of light and strange glowing orbs flashing through the night sky. It is said that residents of Dutch ancestry often sense a supernatural presence lingering around their homes or feel "cold spots," places with a drop in temperature that is thought to be the psychic aftermath in a location where violence has occurred. Some have also reported the removal and eventual return of objects in their homes and, more frightening, feeling as if they were being strangled by ghostly hands.

Not all of New Castle's spirits have been in residence for hundreds of years. In the late twentieth century, a blaze broke out in the development called **Overview Gardens,** in a house on Karlyn Street. The fire reportedly swept through the attic and killed three children who were sleeping there. The house was later renovated, but to this day, three mischievous spirits apparently still linger within. Light footsteps are frequently heard running up and down the stairs, radio stations suddenly change without warning, keys disappear, and doors open and close on their own.

The Twenty-First Century

LIKE MOST AMERICAN STATES, DELAWARE IS A MELTING POT OF DIVERSE ethnic groups, ranging from the early English settlers to more recent immigrants from India and Asia. Residents of the First State share common concerns with many people nationwide about devastating hurricanes, war in the Middle East, and other social issues. At the same time, Delaware's unique identity is preserved through its folk tales and stories of the supernatural, which are regularly supplemented by a growing number of urban legends. Without fail, a new story can be told about almost any quiet stretch of beach or bridge that spans a wooded glen. Newcomers to the state may be a little dismayed to discover that the spectral population of Delaware is growing annually almost as fast as the living one.

Supernatural "Hailstones"

The phenomenon first happened about ten years ago, when Jim and Sally bought a small beachfront cottage in Rehoboth. They were so proud of the fact that they could finally afford a vacation home of their own that they didn't raise too many questions as to why the well-kept property had been on the market four times in the past eight years. But they hadn't stayed there for long when they discovered why the quaint two-bedroom house had changed hands so many times. As Sally tells the story:

It began a little after midnight. Jim and I are both pretty sound sleepers, but our bedroom there is on the second floor, and there was no way we were going to sleep through what sounded at first like a violent hailstorm bouncing off the tin roof. I mean, for a minute or so, I expected to see huge balls of ice come crashing through the windows. But after a few minutes, I rose and went to the window, and there wasn't a cloud in the sky. The sound continued to pound the roof for another few minutes, then stopped as abruptly as it started. We didn't think much more about it until the following day. That was when, during a conversation with our new neighbors, we learned that our house was known locally as the Stone House. Apparently, the phenomenon of invisible stones rattling down the cottage roof was a story that had been passed down locally for years by some of the old-timers.

Although they have not yet learned why the cottage is annually assaulted by a barrage of stones, the owners have decided to keep the property. They feel it's worth sacrificing one night's sleep in order to enjoy proximity to the coastline. There have been no other supernatural manifestations during their three weeks' vacation time each year. They occasionally toy with the idea of visiting the house at a different time, but they're busy professionals and it's not easy to change their schedules, though they admit to being curious to try it, just to see if the incident occurs only during a certain time of year or is perhaps caused by their presence.

More UFO Sightings

In the summer of 2001, a pilot told authorities he saw a blue, egg-shaped object emitting a trail of white vapor moving north very quickly up U.S. Route 13 in northern Delaware. After a few minutes, it disappeared behind some clouds, but as far as the pilot was concerned, the object was definitely not an airplane.

There were almost simultaneous sightings of unidentified flying objects on the same night in 2002 in Slaughter Beach, Frankford, and Newport. The witnesses to the Slaughter Beach UFO stated that two bright lights appeared in the night sky, traveling at high rates of speed. At first the witnesses thought they were seeing shooting stars—until the lights turned and sped upward before falling again toward the water. In Frankford, a family's sleep was disrupted by a bright light streaming in through their bedroom windows. As they watched, the light played through the woods behind their home before it ultimately sped away into the sky. The two witnesses to the Newport incident were out walking their dog when they spotted a large, oval object with a reflective surface moving slowly overhead before it took off into the clouds.

In the fall of 2002, a man was driving south past the Dover Air Force Base when he pulled over near a large field to make a cell phone call. During his conversation, he noticed bright lights in the field where none had been visible just moments before. As he watched in amazement, a triangular object emitting a luminous glow rose silently and hovered briefly more than two hundred feet above the ground. After a few minutes, it turned slowly and flew northeast. Although the witness attempted to follow, the craft soon disappeared over a clump of trees. When he later discussed the sighting with family members, he learned that a similar object had appeared in that same area two years before.

On a cold night in the winter of 2004, an Elsmere resident who was returning home from shopping exited his car to find three UFOs flying silently overhead in a straight line. The witness said they had no apparent lights, and after a few minutes, they broke formation and flew swiftly away. The man had been brought up in a military household and adamantly declared that the aircraft were not of human design.

Since then, UFO sightings continue to be reported from various portions of the state—perhaps keeping tabs on what is going on at Dover Air Force Base and other government facilities located there?

Imprisoned Spirits

Patty Cannon is not the only spectral being said to haunt the Women's Correctional Institute in New Castle, which was built on top of the town's potter's field in the early nineteenth century. Witnesses have heard several spirits there: Seven-year-old Jamie can still be heard crying for her mother in the vicinity of the jail's shower room. The voices of other children can be heard in the halls, in addition to the raised voices of a woman and a man, apparently engaged in a dispute.

Fiddler at the Bridge

Two miles south of St. Georges Bridge was another crossing called Scott Run, often used by area residents in early nineteenth century. To entertain passersby, an old slave known as Jacob would sit by the bridge and play a tune for anyone who cared to listen. Unfortunately, he displeased his master one day and was beaten so badly as punishment that he died shortly afterward. But his spirit apparently returned to the one spot where he happily made music. It is said that anyone who lingers in the vicinity of the bridge can hear Jacob still playing to this day, merrily fiddling a tune for those who are traveling by.

Canal Collision

More than three hundred years ago, Lord Baltimore's surveyor, Augustine Herman, envisioned a canal connecting the Delaware Bay to the Chesapeake River. Such an innovation would eliminate the need to travel all the way around the peninsula, saving (at that time) weeks of sailing. More than a century and a half passed, however, before Herman's proposal became a reality. Construction on the Chesapeake and Delaware (C&D) Canal began in the 1820s; for five years, workmen dug the fourteen-mile link between St. Georges Meadow in Delaware and Maryland's Back Creek.

Once opened, the C&D Canal was an immediate success. Although the privately owned company that ran the canal charged tolls for its use, the C&D was immensely popular with farmers and merchants who needed a quick way to transport their goods to market. By 1833, the canal had become a favorite steamship excursion between Philadelphia and Baltimore. Early in the twentieth century, the canal was purchased and enlarged by the federal government. Today it is maintained by the Army Corps of Engineers and remains a major artery for all types of water traffic—and all sorts of spectral life.

Since its opening, the C&D Canal has witnessed a number of drownings, some easily explainable, some less so. One that still puzzles authorities is the death of an Elkton man who was last seen alive in March 1999, pulling into a friend's driveway. Six weeks later, his body was discovered in the canal east of Chesapeake City.

Over the years, there have also been reports of crewmen mysteriously disappearing from their vessels, never to be seen again . . . at least, not while they are still alive. One of the worst disasters that affected the canal in recent years was the collision of the tugboat *Swift* and a carrier ship, the *A. V. Kastner,* which occurred just west of the C&D. Although the vessels apparently had agreed to pass one another during an earlier radioed conversation, the captain and three crew members of the *Swift* were killed as the tugboat sank to the bottom of the channel. The canal remained closed for weeks while authorities conducted an investigation of the accident.

Although water traffic on the C&D Canal is heavy once again, there are occasional lulls late at night. That's when some residents who live near the water say they can hear the sound of voices calling for help or see the outline of an old-time sailing ship passing by. Occasionally, on foggy nights, they can hear in the distance the sound of horns blaring and metal screeching, as though the two ships are reenacting their fatal collision.

Firehouse Foe

The brave firefighters of Christiana Engine Company no. 3 in Newark sometimes find themselves confronted by a foe that can't be doused by water from a hose. An evil presence that sometimes appears in shadowy form apparently haunts the hallway leading to the engineer's room in the station house. Lurking in the hallway apparently is all the ghost can do, however, since another presence, radiating benevolence, confines it to that space. Although neither spirit manifests itself very often, it is reported that there is a sensation of constant, invisible battle.

The Specters of Smyrna

The town of Smyrna has its share of ghostly residents. It is believed that the Native American population that once lived in the area of Black Diamond Road haunts the housing developments that sprang up here in recent years. The houses apparently were built on top of an Indian burial ground, and photographs taken there frequently show orbs and misty images that appear to be Native Americans hovering in the background.

Smyrna is also home to the Blevins House, where sightings of both human and animal spirits have been reported, including an invisible barking dog, a faceless ghost that peers in through the windows, and another that wanders the grounds in search of his missing head.

Another spectral resident of Smyrna lives on Union Street, where homeowners have sighted a girl in a white dress floating down hallways. When she appears, chairs move, household items disappear, and electrical appliances suddenly turn on. No one is sure of what keeps her hovering around, but the child who haunts Vela House is there for a specific tragic reason. Local residents say that he was bound by his father, who then forced gasoline down his throat and set the boy on fire. The child's spirit is sometimes seen walking around the house, carrying a funnel, or appears reflected briefly in a mirror when one first enters a room.

Respect for the Dead

Lenni-Lenape spirits are said to haunt the sands of Milford Neck, where an archaeological excavation has exposed more than a hundred Native American graves to public view. Personal effects that were buried with the bodies more than a thousand years ago have also been placed on display. Some believe that Dutch soldiers massacred the Lenni-Lenape population that once lived here, and as a result, their ghosts linger at the site. Others think the specters haunt the region because they feel their sacred burial ground has been desecrated.

Pass Quickly by Pike Creek

Strange things have reportedly happened at night on the isolated stretch of road that passes Pike Creek near Newark. People have heard bloodcurdling screams. Unidentified creatures have been seen chasing after cars. Even the trees that line the road seem as if they would prefer to fall and trap unsuspecting travelers there. One tree is said to have become the final resting place of an abandoned infant. Anyone who is foolish enough to stop near it for any length of time can hear the sound of a baby still crying in the dark.

Cry Baby Ghosts

Cry Baby Bridge is a seemingly strange name for a wooden bridge over a creek in a peaceful pastoral setting. That's what Smyrna residents call this Sandtown location, which is not so peaceful after dark. The night air fills with whispers, strange lights glow in the forest, and a silent figure can be seen standing among the trees. The fifty-foot-long bridge is reportedly haunted by a baby whose teenage mother threw him off the bridge because he was born with physical deformities. The infant died, but his spirit is said to haunt the location. The baby's ghost is credited with knocking over trees, which have fallen near the bridge, when he throws a tantrum crying for his mother. Teenagers looking for a place to party have been sobered when their vehicles began to move without drivers or car doors locked and windows rolled themselves up and down. The story of Newark's Boogie Run Baby bears a strong resemblance to that of Smyrna's Cry Baby Bridge. Boogie Run, also known as Creek Road, was once an isolated wooded spot where teenagers partied, building bonfires and skinny-dipping by moonlight. But some local residents say that in the 1950s, it was also the place where a deranged woman abandoned her baby, and that when the moon is full, the sound of the Boogie Run Baby crying still echoes through the woods.

The Witch's Tree

The Witch's Tree in Selbyville is said to be the site of frequent supernatural manifestations, perhaps caused by the pagan rituals once held there. Although the tree is virtually inaccessible, with a forest on one side and a wide ditch on the other, an old truck is often seen parked nearby with a man sitting inside it, reading a newspaper. On other occasions, people have heard the sounds of a truck engine, a man mumbling, a woman crying, and dogs barking.

Morris Farm

A trail from Broadkill Beach Road at the Prime Hook Wildlife Refuge supposedly leads to a farm once owned by the Jonathan J. Morris family. After the farm burned a number of years ago, hikers reported supernatural voices coming from the family cemetery located at the site.

Slaughter Beach

The origins of Slaughter Beach's place name are lost in Delaware's past, but one plausible explanation is still recalled by some area residents. In Colonial times, the relationship between the colonists and Native Americans had deteriorated to the point where combat seemed inevitable. One immigrant named Brabant decided to take drastic action before a massacre could occur. Inviting the local Indian chiefs to a meeting on the beach, Brabant warned them that they would soon hear the voice of the Great Spirit, who would punish those who intended harm to the settlers. With that, he suddenly fired a cannon into their midst, wounding or killing a number of those present. The chiefs, intimidated by Brabant's obvious influence over the deities, did as they were told. But though he ensured the peace—at least temporarily—for the colonists, Brabant's victims did not rest easily. For generations, the cries of the murdered Indians were heard at night on Slaughter Beach.

A more recent account of supernatural activity includes a lone ghost who is said to haunt the marshes near Slaughter Neck Ditch at Slaughter Beach. As the story goes, a local man walked into the marshes and committed suicide with a gun after he lost his family and all his material possessions in a hurricane. His ghost is said to reappear whenever violent storms threaten the coast.

The Girl of the Dunes

Beaches lure people for all kinds of reasons. Some find the rush of the water against to shoreline to be tranquil and relaxing. Others enjoy the opportunity to socialize while they work on a tan. But for some, the coast holds an attraction of another kind—one that is not dispelled simply by death.

The girl who haunts the dunes at Indian River Inlet at the Delaware Seashore State Park apparently is compelled to frequent the beach there. Like New Jersey's "Woman in White," she seems destined to spend the afterlife haunting this particular section of the coast. In *Terrifying Tales 2 of the Beaches and Bays*, Ed Okonowicz states that the specter's real name is Molly McGwinn, but she is also known locally by several different names, including Ghost Girl, Shipwreck Sally, and Dune Demon.

For more than a hundred years, Molly has been seen on numerous occasions by both visitors and the staff of the Indian River Life Saving Station, which was built in 1876 by the United States Life-Saving Service. According to Okonowicz, she frequently appears along the high dunes near the station after the sun goes down. Is it possible that Molly was one of the numerous unfortunates who never made it to shore when their ship sank?

It seems her story is a little more complicated than that.

As Okonowicz further explains in his book, Molly McGwinn may have been an Irish immigrant who was the indentured servant of a crew of wreckers, led by a man named Harwell. The wreckers were unscrupulous land pirates who lured hapless ships close to shore in order to strip the foundering vessel, its crew, and its passengers of any money or valuables that washed to shore. It may have been Molly's job to watch for passing ships from the top of the dunes and signal the ships with a lantern that lured them dangerously close to the coast.

Unlike the rest of the crew, however, Molly seemed to have had a conscience. She longed to escape from the wreckers but was unable to find the courage to break away. When she fell in love with a young Englishman named Nathan, Molly realized that she might finally have a chance to start a new life. Although he was scheduled to return to England shortly after they met, Nathan promised they would be wed when he returned in six months' time. Molly promised to wait and reluctantly waved good-bye as her lover set sail for home.

In the weeks that followed, Molly found herself watching the coast at every opportunity, hoping that each passing ship was the one carrying Nathan back to Delaware. But when six months passed, she despaired that her lover would ever return to rescue her. She resolved that if he did not come back before winter, she would drown herself rather than remain a part of Harwell's crew.

Then one fateful night, she was ordered to her post on top of the dunes and signaled a ship that soon crashed against the coastline. Her thoughts far away, Molly watched uninterestedly as the crew rapidly went to work. As two of the men quarreled over their bounty, however, she was stunned to recognize a familiar form that had washed up on the shore. It was Nathan. And thanks to her, he was dead.

With a cry of grief, Molly threw herself into the surf. Weighted down by her gown, she drowned beneath the waves. But she was not destined to rest peacefully. By the 1890s, staff at the lifesaving station were surprised to see the figure of a young woman carrying a lantern standing watch on the dunes at night. Perhaps she is hoping that if she keeps a faithful vigil, Nathan will find her someday. Then they will finally be able to start their new life together.

The Academic Ghost

The same Mr. Bancroft who started the Bancroft Academy in Wilmington in the nineteenth century apparently is still reluctant to leave the premises where he spent so many years of his life. Students have reported that the lights in the second-floor girls' bathroom will suddenly go out, and anyone who makes the mistake of staring into a mirror will see his glowing red eyes staring back. He has also made his presence known on Friday the thirteenth; any student who knocks on the bathroom wall on that day will hear Mr. Bancroft respond in kind.

Bellevue Mansion

Mysterious events are said to happen regularly in the upstairs rooms of the Bellevue Mansion in Wilmington, another du Pont family home. As lights flicker and dining-room chairs rearrange themselves, the sound of eerie laughter or horrible screams can be heard echoing through the house.

Lemonade Mullery

Anything can happen on a visit to the Dead President's Tavern on Union Street in Wilmington, a two hundred-year-old pub that apparently has a resident poltergeist. Besides flinging dishes through the air and screaming loudly at the most unexpected moments, dominos have been seen floating around the recreation room. These incidents are often credited to the ghost of Lemonade

Mullery, a steady customer of the tavern in the 1950s and '60s who doesn't seem to realize that—for him—last call was a long time ago. Mullery's spirit apparently lingers at the tavern because he died of a broken neck after he slipped and fell in a puddle of urine on the men's room floor. Although his presence can still be felt there, he hasn't discouraged customers, who still flock to the pub.

A Very Dedicated Cast

The Everett Theater in Middletown has been the home of performers so dedicated to their craft that they hover there even after death. Closed for more than fifty years after it was built in 1922, the theater was resurrected in 1983 as a local playhouse. Modern-day actors have frequently found they aren't alone as they wait to perform, however. Misty figures have been seen loitering in the corridors backstage, and the sound of soft laughter is occasionally heard behind the scenes. Performers have reported the disappearance of props and the touch of icy fingers before they step onstage. Perhaps the extra cast members were part of the company that once performed in the opera house that stood on the site where the Everett was built. Theater tradition notes that most actors were notoriously superstitious. They usually had difficulty adapting to change—whether in the script or with the unexpected arrival of the afterlife. Perhaps that is why even after the opera house burned, some of the performers have remained behind, still waiting to take that final bow.

Unlucky Thirteen

In the early 1960s, the Casper family bought a three-story house in Felton once known as the Fountain House Hotel. Built in 1853, the Fountain House was at one time a house of ill repute. The Caspers converted it into the G&B Market, and today it still serves the community in that capacity. But customers occasionally find themselves getting a little more than they ordered, thanks to the building's early occupants.

According to the owners, ghostly "ladies of the night" still promenade along the upper corridors and in the kitchen. Others have been seen sitting on residents' beds, smiling. The sound of chains dragging through the halls, cold drafts, and a glowing orb have also been reported there. Some of the spectral energy may be related to the fact that there are thirteen rooms on the third floor, which still bear the numbers on the doors from the "good old days."

The building may not be a market much longer; the owners have discussed selling the property to make room for a new firehouse. It is doubtful, however, that the change will dispel the phantom occupants, who have lingered there for more than 150 years.

The Phantom Lighthouse Keeper

Settled in the seventeenth century, Fenwick Island is a peaceful shore community in southeastern Delaware. It was once claimed that the island was discovered by a man named Thomas Fenwick after he was thrown overboard by a band of pirates. For generations, life on the island was quite simple, with primitive living conditions, but that was the way year-round residents preferred it, and the community's three hundred permanent residents today are proud of the island's distinctly noncommercial atmosphere, broad beaches, and peaceful atmosphere. A lighthouse was constructed on the island in 1856. One young visitor who stayed with relatives on the island in the early 1980s has decidedly colorful memories of the town and its lighthouses:

> I was about twelve, and my cousins Mary and Michael were twelve and fourteen, the summer I spent two weeks with them at the shore. Like all kids, we enjoyed nothing more than splashing in the waves and playing Frisbee on the beach during the day. At night, we'd roast hot dogs and marshmallows and shiver with delight as we tried to see who could make up the most outrageous ghost stories. Michael usually won, because most of his stories centered around a phantom lighthouse keeper who, he claimed, still haunted the Fenwick Island Lighthouse.
>
> One night, after I had been there for a few days, Mary dug out an old Ouija board, and that became our newest obsession. Every evening, we'd sit out on an old picnic table parked in a corner of the back patio and try our best to contact the spirits. To make sure his sister and I stayed thoroughly frightened, Michael would periodically try to communicate with the ghost of the lighthouse keeper. He said the man had died a sudden and mysterious death

about fifty years earlier, inside the tall structure, which was just a couple miles from my aunt and uncle's summer home. Halfway through just about every session, we'd get silly and start shoving the planchette around before finally giving up for the night.

One night, though, I'll never forget. It was warm, a little overcast, but a beautiful full moon hung over the water. Of course, we couldn't stay inside on a night like that, so we grabbed the Ouija board and headed for our favorite spot in the backyard. We each placed two fingers on the planchette, and Michael called out, "Oh, spirit of the lighthouse, please speak to us. Please tell us if you're out there . . ."

At first nothing happened. But then Mary and I both gasped as the planchette started to move beneath our fingers almost as if in response to his words. Suddenly, before we could do or say anything else, the thing began to spin madly and after a minute or so seemed to jump straight off the board. As Michael went to retrieve it, he stopped cold. Mary and I followed his gaze into the distance, and there, from within a small window on an upper story of the lighthouse, we could see a glow where it had previously been dark. We knew that was wrong. Nobody—nothing—was supposed to be in the lighthouse anymore. Wordlessly, we fled back into the household, leaving the Ouija board outside. When we later told the adults about what we had seen, Uncle Ralph just laughed and said it was probably the reflection of the moonlight against the outside of the lighthouse. But when I think back to that night, and the way the light seemed to glow from within the building, I wish I could say I was as sure as he had been about what we had seen.

Beware of Bigfoot

Over the years, Delaware residents have occasionally reported seeing New Jersey's notorious Jersey Devil flying by. The Devil, it seems, has been spotted visiting such faraway locations as Texas and Louisiana, so he likely would not be fazed by a short trip across the bay. Though Delaware doesn't have an "official" state monster like New Jersey's Jersey Devil, travelers sometimes hear locals refer to a creature known as the Cape Henlopen Devil, who is jokingly called the Jersey Devil's offspring. Little information exists on the Cape Henlopen Devil, but another strange creature apparently roams the First State's woods.

According to reports from the Bigfoot Research Organization website, there have been two sightings of the famous monster in Delaware in recent years, even though his favorite stomping grounds are supposed to be in the West. The first occurred in June 2003 near the town of Cool Spring in Sussex County. A man and his eighteen-year-old son had left Cape Henlopen State Park at about 1:30 in the morning, after a long day of fishing. They turned west onto State Route 404, and as there was very little traffic, the man drove with his high beams on and set the cruise control.

They crossed through quiet farm country, dotted by stands of trees, down a wooded road whose surface was occasionally covered by a soft ground haze. The peace of early morning was suddenly shattered when a deer flashed across the road in front of them. The man braked in time, but they proceeded slowly after that just in case more deer were nearby. A few minutes later, they observed movement among the trees—but this time it wasn't deer. Stunned, the father and son watched as two forms appeared by the roadside, walking on two feet—but decidedly not human. The man braked, and they watched as the two figures disappeared into the forest. They later described the larger of the two creatures as more than six feet in height, and its companion at least a foot shorter, and they said both were much too hairy to be human beings.

Six months later, just a few miles away, near Georgetown, a lone traveler saw a similar creature on his way home from class one night. He recalled that it was cold and moonless as he detoured down a rural country road. He was approaching a crossroads when he saw a huge form, roughly seven feet tall, standing next to a utility pole. Surprised to see someone standing in the middle of nowhere, the young student decided to take a closer look at the figure by the side of the road. As he slowed his car, he realized that the creature could not possible be human. Its entire body appeared to be covered in thick black hair, and the hair on its head rose to a point. Real fear did not set in, however, until the creature turned and their gaze connected. According to the report filed with the website, the young man wished that someone else had been present at the encounter to see this mysterious being.

Headless Specters

Some Newark residents tell a completely different tale about a headless specter on Cooch's Bridge, where the famous Revolutionary War battle occurred. In the 1950s, a motorcycle rider is said to have had an accident on the bridge in which he lost his head. Legend has it that at midnight, during the full moon, a ghostly rider returns to the bridge in an effort to find his missing head.

Drivers are sometimes warned to be extremely cautious when traveling U.S. Route 113 near the Delaware State Forest at night. There have been reports of a headless figure seen walking along the roadside. Could this have contributed to the high rate of accidents that have occurred on this stretch of road?

The Brandywine Werewolf

Does a werewolf haunt the region of the creek at Brandywine State Park? The story goes that a scout named Gil Thoreau was exploring the northern section of Delaware in the 1830s, when he was attacked and bitten by a wild creature. His ghost, nicknamed the Red Fox Dog, has haunted the site ever since.

Flying Solo

Although no one has ever been able to learn the reason why, it is said that the ghost of World War I flying ace Eddie Rickenbacker haunts a stretch of Bethany Beach. Perhaps Rickenbacker, who had become one of America's first race-car drivers before joining the military, is trying to find his way to Dover Downs to see how modern race cars perform.

Unwelcome Guests

The plain white farmhouse with the sagging front porch shows signs of age: the paint is peeling, the gingerbread is gone, and a step is missing from the back stairs. First built in the early 1900s outside of Andrewsville, it sits in the middle of a cluster of farm buildings that range from an aged barn to a modern, vinyl-covered storage shed at the rear of the property. Although family-owned for generations, the house recently was sold to new owners who had hoped to settle into a quiet life in the country. They have changed their minds about restoring the farmhouse to its original condition, however. It seems that some of the previous occupants have made the new owners feel like unwelcome guests in their own house.

Although nothing has occurred to disturb their tranquility during the daylight hours, the current owners report that the ghosts are not shy about making their presence known at any time between midnight and dawn. Pots and pans mysteriously clatter in kitchen cabinets long after the couple has retired for the night. Footsteps can be heard repeatedly crossing the attic, although no flooring runs the length of the space. Then there is periodic angry banging on the back door, although no one is there when they look.

The new owners might have been able to tolerate all of these supernatural experiences but for one that was the most frightening—and heartbreaking—of all. At least once a week since they took possession of the house, they have heard the sound of a child crying quietly in one of the upstairs bedrooms. Whenever they investigate, the crying evaporates on a cool breath of air, even when the windows are closed. Although that is the phenomenon they hear the least, it has been the final straw that has led the couple to look elsewhere for a quiet countryside retreat. Are they curious about the restless spirits who don't seem to want to share their abode? Of course, but husband and wife agree that they no longer prefer to learn more about their "roommates" firsthand.

Hunting for Haunts

No ONE REALLY KNOWS WHY THERE HAS BEEN A RECENT UPSURGE OF interest in learning more about paranormal phenomena. And Delaware residents have been no exception. Over the years, a number of paranormal investigation groups have been organized there to help residents who are plagued by restless spirits. Other agencies from outside the First State have also conducted research into haunted structures there. One now-defunct organization that had some success with its investigations was a branch of the Ghost Chasers Society, an organization formed in 1955, which was once headquartered in Little Creek. Among the phenomena that members witnessed were a Kent County ghost that liked to rearrange table settings after the restaurant it haunted closed for the night, the unexplained sound of whistling in a cemetery, and the spirit of a murder victim at a farmhouse who attempted to communicate by moving objects around. Like all such groups, the Ghost Chasers did not charge concerned citizens for their investigations, preferring simply to record and share whatever information they discovered at a site.

Some area organizations actively involved in paranormal research include South Jersey Paranormal Research, South Jersey Ghost Research, and the New Jersey Ghost Research organization. Although not based in Delaware, members have traveled there to investigate supernatural phenomena and frequently conduct seminars for novices interested in learning more about the subject. Inspired by a number of books and magazines on the subject, a lot of people are staking out graveyards and old buildings in hopes of finding a ghost or some other evidence of spectral activity.

Amateur paranormal investigators should always proceed with caution when searching for evidence of the supernatural. Respect No Trespassing signs, which might be posted because a building is physically unsound. Also, entering a property without express written permission of the owner could lead to trouble with local authorities. Always carry identification and letters of permission, as well as essential equipment such as a flashlight, tape recorder, extra batteries, and log book. Whenever possible, visit potential sites in the daytime first to make sure you will not run into unexpected obstacles after dark. Above all, it is important to stay focused on the work at hand—if you allow yourself to be distracted by earthly sources, you likely will find it difficult to determine the presence of any spectral beings. To learn more about proper paranormal investigation procedures, visit any of the numerous websites dedicated to this subject, such as www.sjgr.org, www.njghs.net, www.njghostresearch.org, or www.sjpr.com.

If this book has piqued your curiosity about the First State's haunted history, check out the following websites to learn a little more about what there is to see in Delaware on the supernatural level: www.dawghouse.topcities.com, www.angelfire.com, www.haunted-places.com, www.prairieghosts.com, www.theshadowlands.net, www.paranormalnews.com, and the "Haunted Delaware Directory," which can be found at www.pages.zdnet.com. Better yet, take some time to see firsthand the places where the ghosts and legends reside. In nearly any historic city or charming rural town, you'll find some locals with supernatural tales to tell. In the fall, it's easy to find information on ghost walks or ghost tours of historic sites such as Fort Delaware.

When you're touring haunted Delaware, let the many supernatural myths, legends, and other scary tales serve as a reminder to be a little more careful of the unknown—especially after dark. If you think that tree-lined country road looks peaceful, that charming stranger may just be lost and in need of directions, or that delightful old house seems like a place you just have to explore . . .

Just remember, appearances can be deceiving!

Bibliography

Books

Dorson, Richard M. *American Folklore*. Chicago: University of Chicago Press, 1959.

Federal Writers Project. *Delaware: A Guide to the First State*. New York: Hastings House, 1938.

Foulke, Patricia, and Robert Foulke. *Colonial America: A Traveler's Guide*. Old Saybrook, CT: Globe Pequot Press, 1995.

Frank, Bill. *Bill Frank's Delaware*. Wilmington: Middle Atlantic Press, 1987.

Bill Frank Collection, box 4, folder 31, Historical Society of Delaware, Dover.

Guiley, Rosemary Ellen. *The Encyclopedia of Ghosts and Spirits*. New York: Facts on File, 1992.

Hauck, Dennis. *Haunted Places: Ghost Abodes, Sacred Sites, UFO Landings, and Other Supernatural Locations*. New York: Penguin Book, 1994.

Hoffecker, Carol E. *Delaware: A Bicentennial History*. New York: W. W. Norton & Co., 1977.

Jeffrey, Adi-Kent Thomas. *Ghosts in the Valley*. Warminster, PA: Hampton Publishing Co., 1971.

Martin, Roger. *Tales of Delaware: "Faces and Places."* N.p.: Roger A. Martin, 1991.

Miller, Joanne, ed. *Moon Handbooks: Maryland & Delaware*. Avalon Travel, 2004.

Mobil Travel Guide 2004: Mid-Atlantic. Park Ridge, IL: Exxon-Mobil Travel Publications, Rand-McNally & Company, 2004.

Munroe, John A. *Colonial Delaware: A History*. Milwood, NY: KTO Press, 1978.

Norman, Michael, and Beth Scott. *Haunted Heritage*. Tom Doherty Associates LLC, 2002.

Okonowicz, Ed. *Pulling Back the Curtain: True Stories of Ghosts on the Delmarva Peninsula,* vol. 1. Elkton, MD: Myst & Lace Publishers, 1994.

———. *Terrifying Tales 2 of the Beaches and Bays.* Elkton, MD: Myst & Lace Publishers, 2001.

———. *Welcome Inn: Haunted Inns, Restaurants, and Museums,* vol. 3. Elkton, MD: Myst & Lace Publishers, 1995.

Pickering, David. *Cassell Dictionary of Superstitions.* London: Cassell Wellington House, 1995.

Porter, Glenn. *The Workers' World at Hagley.* Wilmington, DE: Hagley Museum and Library, 1992.

Pyle, Howard. *Howard Pyle's Book of Pirates: Fiction, Fact and Fancy Concerning the Buccaneers and Marooners of the Spanish Main.* Electronic Text Center, University of Virginia Library, etext.lib.virginia.edu/tox/modeng/public/PylPira.html.

Seibold, David J., and Charles J. Adams III. *Ghost Stories of the Delaware Coast.* Reading, PA: Exeter House Books, 2000.

Skinner, Charles M. *American Myths and Legends.* Detroit: Gale Research Company, 1974.

Townsend, George Alfred. *The Entailed Hat.* Cambridge, MD: Tidewater Publishers, 1955.

Trapani, Bob Jr. *Lighthouses of New Jersey and Delaware: History, Mystery, Legends and Lore.* Elkton, MD: Myst & Lace Publishers, 2005.

Woods, Caroline. *Haunted Delaware: Delightfully Dreadful Legends of the First State* Haverford, PA: Infinity Publishing, 2000.

Online Resources
(in order of story)

"Introduction." *Delaware History Online.* Retrieved January 21, 2005. www.hsd.org.

"Native American Tales." *Lores.* Retrieved January 18, 2005. www.zicahota.com.

"Cheney Clow's Rebellion." *Kent Farm.* Retrieved July 10, 2005. www.doverpost.com.

"Sunken Ships and Pirate Treasure." *Pirates: Blueskin the Pirate.* Retrieved January 24, 2005. skullandcrossbones.org.

"Within Winterthur." *About Winterthur.* Retrieved May 30, 2005. www.winterthur.org.

"Fortress of Fear." *Andersonville of the North: The Ghosts on Pea Patch Island.* Retrieved January 4, 2005. www.suite101.com.

"Picture Perfect." *The Darley House.* Retrieved July 18, 2005. www.state.de.us.

Bibliography

"Garfield's Ghost." *Paranormal News—Your Source for UFO and Paranormal Related Information.* Retrieved May 13, 2005. www.paranormalnews.com.

"Ghostly Writing." *Spirit Writing.* Retrieved July 8, 2005. www.prairieghosts.com.

"The Seven Whistlers and the Merman." *Pals of the Merman.* Retrieved July 15, 2005. www.roadsideamerica.com.

"Wartime Memories." *The Air Mobility Command Museum home page.* Retrieved July 13, 2005. www.amcmuseum.org.

"Fairy Sightings." *Fairy Gardens-Youth Fairy Sightings.* Retrieved July 15, 2005. www.fairygardens.com.

"The Silk King." *CPAmedia.com: Jim Thompson—Thailand's Silk King.* Retrieved July 13, 2005. www.cpamedia.com.

"UFO Sightings." *Article_DelawareUFO1905.* Retrieved January 18, 2005. www.aliendave.com.

"Some Haunted Houses and Other Scary Places." *Shadowlands Haunted Places Index.* Retrieved January 15, 2005. http://theshadowlands.net.

"Beware of Bigfoot." *BFRO Report 6740.* Retrieved February 7, 2005. www.bfro.net.

"Hunting for Haunts." *Ghost Chasers on the Lookout in Delaware (Fall 1992).* Retrieved May 17, 2005. www.udel.edu; *Pre-Ghost Hunting Tips.* Retrieved July 17, 2005. www.mysticalblaze.com.

Acknowledgments

I THANK MY TALENTED EDITOR, KYLE WEAVER, FOR ALL HIS GOOD ADVICE and support, and his assistant, Amy Cooper, who has a gift for detail; Heather Adel, a consummate artist whose illustrations bring the stories to life; my friend Charles A. Stansfield Jr., who gave me the encouragement I needed to "fly solo"; Ed Okonowicz, author and storyteller extraordinaire, who graciously shared tales of Delaware's supernatural past; author Bob Trapani Jr., who generously provided much-needed insight on the history and mystery of lighthouses; my invaluable research assistant, Cheryl Hendry; Marjorie McNinch, reference archivist at the Hagley Museum and Library; Michael Leister, director of the Air Mobility Command Museum; the countless wizards of the Internet, whose wondrous sites are filled with arcane knowledge; and the dedicated staff of the Vineland Public Library, who continue to conjure much-needed reference sources from the invisible world of interlibrary loan.

About the Author

Dale Wettstein/Steelman Photos

SOUTH JERSEY NATIVE PATRICIA A. MARTINELLI IS A VETERAN FREELANCE writer whose interests include history and supernatural phenomena. Over the years, her work has appeared in numerous regional newspapers and national magazines. In 2004, she collaborated with Charles A. Stansfield Jr. on a collection of ghost stories titled *Haunted New Jersey: Ghosts and Strange Phenomena of the Garden State*. The success of that book inspired Martinelli to look further afield to her first solo project. The current volume offers a varied selection of classic folktales, urban legends, and stories of the supernatural from throughout Delaware.